The BIG DAY

AF794716

The BIG DAY

Saying "I Do"
Only to Discover
I Didn't

LISA CHEEK

SWP

SHE WRITES PRESS

Published in 2026 by
She Writes Press, an imprint of The Stable Book Group

SWP

1569 Solano Ave #546
Berkeley, CA 94707
https://shewritespress.com
Library of Congress Control Number: 2026907590
ISBN: 979-8-89636-306-4
eISBN: 979-8-89636-307-1

Interior Designer: Tabitha Lahr
Line art by Alexandra Navrotska

Printed in the United States

Names and identifying characteristics have been changed to protect the privacy of certain individuals.

For my Great Aunt Betty, who married
my Great Uncle Holman.
When they divorced, she kept me as her family.

CONTENTS

A Note Before We Start 1
Will Ferrell Quote. 3
The Agreement, aka the Vows. 5
The Heat Is On 7
Now What? 10
Should I Stay or Should I Go? 11
There's No Place Like Home. 13
What's in a Name?. 15
Not Until You're Thirty. 16
My Parents 17
Dad's Parents 18
Mom's Parents 20
The French Mistress. 22
The Leak. 23
Dad and Stepmother #1's Wedding 25
Dad and Stepmother #2's Wedding 27
A Conversation with My Dad 28
The Dynamic Duo. 29
Checking It Twice 31
Stepdaddy Mac 34
Stepdaddy Mac's Former Wives 36
Stepdaddy Mac's Advice 37
Stepmother #1's First Marriage. 38
Stepmother #2's First Marriage. 39
Third Time's the Charm 40
Big Johnson and Tammy #1's Marriage . . . 41
Big Johnson and Tammy #2's Marriage . . . 42
Big Johnson's Trying Something New 43
The Wedding Crasher 44

It's Not Lost on Me 46
A Conversation with My Mother. 47
The Colonel and Shirley Johnson
(the Future In-Laws) 48
The Colonel and Shirley's RSVP 49
A False Start. 50
A Holdup. 54
Flower Power 57
Frankie's Glam Gram and
Hurricane Husband. 59
Cher Quote 63
Hunk of Burning Love 65
Stuffed 68
The Great Escape. 71
Firsts. 75
The High School Boyfriend 77
The Musician 83
Big Johnson Wedding Playlist. 86
The Biologist 89
The Actor. 92
The Magician. 98
Steven Wright Quote 101
Rollerblading Dad. 103
Tea Time 107
The Ghoster. 109
The Divorcée 111
The Unavailable Men 112
The Wedding Menu. 115
My Longest Relationship 117

IT Guy 119
My Biggest Worry 121
The Ghoster Returns 122
Mae West Quote 125
The Gym Rat 127
Married to My Job 128
Sibling Math 129
The Introduction 130
The Walk 132
The Meeting 135
The Callback 138
The Ghoster Returns, Again 139
Kendrick Cole Quote 141
The Do-Over 143
The Sleepover 144
The Next Morning 146
The Boy Scout 147
The Rounds 148
The Next Day 149
The Takedown 150
The Poop 151
The Gas Station Attendant 152
The Hustler 153
Peter Pan 156
Keys to the Kingdom 157
Dirty Laundry 158
Meet the Girls 159
A Gift from the Girls 161
Double Take 162

Another Invite 163
A Visit with the Brother 164
Meeting the Johnsons 165
The Naked Truth 166
Something Old 168
Card Shark 169
The Band 171
The Proposal 172
The Celebration Dinner 174
The Ride 179
I Heard It Through the Grapevine 181
Seeing Red 183
Goldilocks 185
Things 186
Blended Family 188
Must-See TV 189
TCB (Taking Care of Business) 190
A Gift for the Guests 192
Hooking Up 193
I Heart You 194
The Ring 196
Let's Get It On 198
Harry Burns Quote 201
Take Two 203
Mr. Incredible Quote 205
The Ghoster's Encore 207
A Note Before We End 208
Acknowledgments 209
About the Author 211

A Note Before We Start

THE BIG DAY is based on my blog, *Becoming Mrs. Johnson.* Getting married for the first time at forty-nine, I wanted to document what it was like for a middle-aged woman.

The Big Day comes from not only that blog but also my memory. Memories that are stored with my own perceptions and misinterpretations of things at the time. I may not be the person to tell you how accurate a moment is, but I will tell you how I experienced it.

Along with my memories, I consulted my grandfather's autobiography, which is his own interpretation of the events in his life.

I've spent most of my life trying to figure out how relationships work. How families get together and stay together is still such a mystery to me. Through writing this story, I did my best to examine my part in each relationship mentioned—knowing I am the common denominator while hoping to become a better person along the way. I am only ever laughing at myself. Please, laugh along with me.

"Before you marry a person, you should first make them use a computer with slow internet to see who they really are."

—Will Ferrell

The Agreement, aka the Vows

WE ARE GATHERED today in the presence of family and friends to share with Lisa and Big Johnson the most important moment in their lives, the choice to be united in marriage.

It has been said that marriage is that relationship in which the independence is equal, dependence mutual, and obligation reciprocal. Lisa and Big Johnson have chosen to bring together the best parts of their individuality, uniting their spirit, talent, and experience to create something better than either of them alone can offer.

By this ceremony you will become husband and wife, but the soul of your marriage depends on the constant renewal of the choices and promises out of love for one another you make today and every day.

Life together will sometimes be playful and effortless, sometimes frustrating and difficult. Each day your relationship will strengthen when you choose to continue to love and honor one another.

Love is something beyond the excitement of romance and being in love. It is a committed, thoughtful decision. Love is nurturing. Love is listening. Love is caring. Love is kind. Love lightens burdens because you divide them, and love intensifies joy because you share it.

It is often said that love makes the world go round. However, without a doubt, it is friendship that keeps our spinning existence on an even keel. True friendship provides so many of the essentials for a happy life—it is the foundation on which to build an enduring relationship, it is the mortar that bonds us together in harmony, and it is the calm, warm protection we sometimes need when the world outside seems cold and chaotic. True friendship nurtures our hopes, supports us in our disappointments, and encourages us to grow to our best potential.

Today, Lisa and Big Johnson pledge to each other not only their love but also strength, warmth, and, most importantly, the fun of true friendship.

The step you are about to take is the most important step into which two human beings can come. It is a union of two people founded upon mutual respect and affection.

It is the wish of everyone here today that your marriage brings you much happiness. Happiness in marriage doesn't just happen, though. You must work on it. Remember to say "I love you," to hold hands whenever you get the chance, and at no time to take the other for granted.

The Heat Is On

IT WAS A record high in the Valley that day—116 degrees in the shade—when Big Johnson popped the question, "Did you get Judge Larson's signature on the marriage certificate before he left?" Sweat streamed down the sides of my new husband's face.

The tiny tiara placed high above my thick ponytail before I walked down the aisle now clung askew just above my right ear, the result of my new brother-in-law trampling on my cathedral-length veil. Using one arm, I straightened out my headwear while holding our ring bearer, Ron Howard, my seventeen-pound strawberry blond poodle-Pomeranian mutt, in my other arm. Ron Howard panted as I jostled him in his black-and-white tuxedo tie.

"Could you move a little closer to the bride?" the photographer directed my dad, who'd brought not one but both of his girlfriends to my long-awaited, much-anticipated nuptials.

In Dad's defense, I invited them both.

"Sir, I need you to stand closer to the mother of the bride."

Dad leaned into frame, doing his best to stand as far away from my mother as he could.

"Now, everyone, *please* scrunch in a little closer?"

Fifteen family members inched toward the middle like an overstuffed suitcase.

"Perfect! Now, on three."

One of the two snaps on my dress's halter popped from the extra poundage I'd put on in the last month. Six weeks earlier, in ballet class, I'd attempted a jeté, followed by an attitude turn into a layout, only to step out sideways on my right foot, fracturing a tiny bone and requiring a walking cast I'd only just taken off that morning, our wedding day.

And now, the sixpence hidden in my misty-blue glittered shoe that my friend Ann had given me to bring good fortune had wedged between two toes on my left foot, bringing on a blister.

"One . . . two . . ."

"I'm done!" Dad shouted as he stomped away, leaving his two girlfriends still smiling, ecstatic to be included in the family portraits.

"Ouch!" Mom screamed in my ear when my stepfather stepped on her toe.

"Perhaps we should give everyone a break," the frustrated photographer suggested.

Family dispersed like cockroaches when the lights come on in the middle of the night. That left just the three of us: Big Johnson, Ron Howard, and me.

"I didn't know the judge needed to sign the marriage certificate?" I said in ignorance. "I've never done this before. You're the one with previous wedding experience."

"Well, we aren't married if the judge didn't sign the license," Big Johnson said, sighing.

"You mean this monumental event that all these people waited almost fifty years for and flew in from all over the world to witness didn't happen?"

I couldn't believe it. On the day I finally said "I do," I found out I didn't.

Now What?

SIGNATURE? NO ONE said anything about a signature. No one said anything about a judge needing to sign the license. How would I know? Big Johnson's been married not once but twice before. Oh, and he's a lawyer. He knows lawyering things.

I whipped the cathedral-length veil off my shoulders and hugged Ron Howard for comfort. He tucked his head under my chin as if we were snuggling up.

Was this what I really wanted? Or had I just been given a sign by not getting the wedding license signed? Maybe it was the heat, the family time, the sixpence, but suddenly, I was questioning . . . was this really what I wanted?

Should I make a run for it?

Be a runaway bride?

Should I Stay or Should I Go?

I'D HAD FIVE marriage proposals before Big Johnson's.

Truth is, I never saw myself doing fifty years with anyone, but since I was about to turn fifty, and I really liked Big Johnson, I thought I could do thirty-five with him. I came up with this number factoring for beyond the average lifespan of a typical American woman.

He really is a capable man if you can look beyond his failure to tell me about getting the signature on the marriage certificate. And my life is way more fun with him in it. It really is. Plus, I wanted to try out this whole partner thing. A long-term relationship was last seen in my early twenties, and I was so young then, that relationship ran on lust and my codependency. I didn't have a clue what real partnership is about.

With a father thrice divorced and a mother living 3,700 miles away, my single-digit years were filled with confusion and judgment. In 1970, I was the only kid in my entire grade school with divorced parents. And a father with custody of two girls on his own back then, well, he was as rare as a pure blue diamond. Have you ever seen one? Exactly.

The stepfamily of my teenage years that followed came with abuse and neglect—so much anger from unfulfilled expectations, grief and sadness, loneliness and bewilderment. Commitment wasn't in our genes. Other than that one relationship in college, nothing lasted longer than six months. Either they would run, or they would ask me to marry them and I would run.

There's No Place Like Home

SIX THIRTY.

Saturday night.

Labor Day weekend.

Sweat poured from my armpits, staining my cream satin halter dress all the way down to its rhinestone waistband.

We spent twenty-five thousand dollars on this wedding. But it was my first and hopefully only marriage, so I'd justified the expense.

I originally proposed City Hall for a quick ceremony. We lived in LA, so perhaps we'd spot a few celebrities between "I dos." I felt too old to have a wedding, but Big Johnson insisted since I'd never been married before, and I wanted to learn the art of compromise. We agreed it would be a budgeted affair.

Big Johnson had just started his own law firm the year before, and whatever savings he had he'd put into building his palatial estate: three stories of dark brown wood and travertine floors. All decorated in nine shades of red, on a vineyard. And yes, a vineyard, in Los Angeles's ever-famous San Fernando Valley. He'd planted 225 Silver Oak Cabernet replacement vines, all tiered with railroad ties, surrounding his humongous house. All the rest was dirt.

With fifteen thousand dollars spent on food and alcohol for seventy-five guests and another six thousand dollars for the rehearsal dinner, a photographer, and a DJ, that left us with four thousand dollars for suiting up Big Johnson and his daughters, Ron Howard's bow tie, tables and chairs, flowers and decorations, and a wineglass remembrance for each guest.

This was far from a budget affair, but we justified it by having the wedding at Big Johnson's vineyard. Even if that meant we needed to hire a valet to get everyone up there.

"Valley girl," here I come.

What's in a Name?

BIG JOHNSON IS a really, really big guy—six foot two, and hovering around three hundred pounds. He played football in high school, which is where he got his nickname.

He keeps asking me to change my name, but again, I've been Lisa Cheek my whole life. I'm not a young bride. I'm forty-nine years old.

What was it about changing my name?

Change is something I know.

I'm good at change.

I've changed schools, states, and countries. I've been a writer, a producer, an editor. I've changed my hair color, address, and job all in the same day. I've even changed what I eat for breakfast. Change is good, right?

"But don't you want to be Mrs. Big Johnson?" he asked me one day.

No! No girl wants to have "Big" in front of her name.

But that got me thinking. Lisa Cheek Johnson really wasn't so bad, at least not compared to Mrs. Big Johnson.

Not Until You're Thirty

I WAS NEVER one of those girls who dreamed of her wedding day. I just didn't get that girl gene.

In fact, the only thing my parents ever said to me about marriage was, "You can't get married until you're thirty."

They'd usually follow it up with, "You can't have a tattoo until you're thirty either."

Advice I had adhered to until now.

Still no ink on my body and now no ink on my marriage certificate.

My Parents

THE FIRST WEDDING I ever attended was my parents'.

Since I still occupied my mother's womb at the time, it was dark and I was too young to have any memories of it. Neither one of my parents ever talked about the festivities, but I have seen a couple of photos.

It was the day after my father graduated from Navy Officer Candidate School. A late-afternoon ceremony at the Chapel by the Sea, a tiny church on the naval base overlooking the water, in Newport, Rhode Island.

Dad donned his navy dress whites. Mom wore a sapphire-blue shift dress that hit just below the knee. Her long ginger-red hair twisted like a pretzel in an updo, the way women wore it in the early '60s, making her hair taller than their small wedding cake, which they cut with a long sword. I know this because I found the obligatory photo of them walking under the arch of swords, a naval tradition, symbolizing the military honors and protection for the new couple.

The next day my father received orders where he was stationed at the Alameda Naval Station in Alameda, California.

No honeymoon that I know of.

Seven months later, I was born in Oakland, California.

Eight years later, they divorced.

Dad's Parents

MY DAD'S PARENTS, Grandma and Granddaddy Cheek, eloped. In her late twenties, Grandma Cheek was way past her prime, having spent her twenties acquiring not only a master's degree but a PhD from Duke University. Unheard of for a woman in her day.

During the Depression, schoolteachers weren't allowed to marry. And at that time, Grandma taught in a one-room schoolhouse in the country in North Carolina. So, when they decided to wed, she and Granddaddy drove south of the border—to Dillon, South Carolina—where they could get a license and be married on the same day. They kept their marriage a secret for a whole year, until Grandma could afford to leave teaching for another job.

If they had a honeymoon, I never heard it mentioned.

Decades later, Grandma taught political science at Duke. Some might say she was a very loud and liberal Democrat. Granddaddy, a quiet, conservative Republican, supervised the post office in Chapel Hill.

Grandma was not only wicked smart but large in stature, five ten and built like a linebacker. Even in her blue floral dresses and low-heeled shoes, she was an imposing figure.

I lived with them for several months around the time of the Watergate scandal and witnessed a lot of yelling. They would have called it "a difference of opinion." I'd made it my mission to complete the Nancy Drew series that summer, so I sat in the living room reading while Walter Cronkite reported on the latest Watergate findings and cover-ups. Grandma chanted, "Tricky Dick, Tricky Dick," while she chased Granddaddy around the living room, down the hall, and into the kitchen, repeating, "He's a crook. I told you he's a crook!"

More than once, Granddaddy made a run for it out the kitchen side door to the backyard where he could smoke his cigar and "get some peace and quiet."

Their different political affiliations built my stuffed animal collection. Grandma gave me a much-loved blue furry donkey with stars and stripes on his tummy, while Granddaddy spent his spare time on the lookout to expand my stuffed elephant family every chance he got.

Grandma and Granddaddy also spent time together at the beach, playing canasta with friends, and were married until Grandma died of Alzheimer's at age eighty-one.

She lived in a nursing home for her last ten years, and Granddaddy visited her every single day until she died.

He did not miss a day.

Not one day.

Mom's Parents

DETAILS OF THE wedding of my maternal grandparents, Gran and Papa, are unknown.

Whenever we visited them, Mom made me ask, "When is your wedding anniversary?"

Every time I asked, they'd change the subject or exit the room, leaving me to tell my mother what she already knew: nothing. Gran and Papa's nuptials were not to be discussed, much less acknowledged or celebrated.

But Papa wrote an autobiography, so some information is known.

Born and raised in London, Gran immigrated to America and married a New Yorker. They had a son. Early in their marriage, her husband was diagnosed with schizophrenia and admitted to a psychiatric hospital.

Papa, born and raised in Stockholm, became a lawyer but felt his opportunities limited, so he packed a bag and moved to the States. Here, he fell in love when he met his first wife, Juanita, from Nicaragua. They married at City Hall and moved to Staten Island, where Papa was happy. They had a son. Right after their baby's birth, Juanita became depressed. Today she would have been diagnosed with postpartum depression. One day, Papa came home from work, smelled gas from the kitchen, and found Juanita and the baby in front of the oven, both dead.

Papa was devastated.

A few years later, Papa met Yvonne, the hostess at Schrafft's restaurant downtown. "Tall and blond with an attractive smile" is how he describes her in his autobiography.

They dated. Yvonne proposed to him. They married in Stockholm.

Two weeks after they returned to New York, Yvonne flew to Reno to file for divorce so she could marry a very wealthy man in the perfumery business. Turned out she married Papa only to get this fragrant man's attention.

In Papa's autobiography, there is a mention of meeting Gran the same year that Yvonne left him. Both divorced, they met at a dinner party.

Papa had recently pitched a Swedish newspaper a story about a trip on the ill-fated Hindenburg and landed the job. There is a small note that Gran saw him off on his Hindenburg assignment, which sounds incredibly romantic to me.

But then there is no mention of Gran again until my mother was born, and not again until after my uncle was born a year later.

According to the rumors I'd heard over the years, my mother and my uncle were born out of wedlock. In 1941, Papa's law firm told him if he wanted to make partner, he needed to make an honest woman out of Gran.

But this is all hearsay.

No evidence to be found.

The French Mistress

MY GREAT-GRANDFATHER on my mother's side had a French mistress.

They had a daughter together.

She and Gran became best friends later in life, introducing me to another whole wonderful French family.

I wish I spoke French.

Thank God they speak English.

The Leak

ON THE MORNING of my big day, I awoke to the sound of the doorbell. It was six thirty.

Big Johnson rolled out of bed, threw on his robe, and hurried down the two flights of stairs, landing at our entryway with its large, wooden, double front doors.

"Good morning! Sorry to wake you, but I was out walking my dog this morning and realized you have a water leak. I think it's coming from the top of your vineyard. It's reached all the way to the end of the street, forming a community pool big enough to swim laps in."

I heard Big Johnson step outside, the front door closing behind him.

Ron Howard, who'd been asleep at my feet, inched his way up the bed and rolled over on his back. With my eyes still closed, I rubbed his tummy.

My goal had been to sleep in this morning. Since we were about to host a wedding at our house, I would be the last guest to leave the party. When I go to someone else's party, I'm the first person to arrive and the first to leave. Having it in our own home? I clearly hadn't thought this whole venue thing through. And now we had a water leak?

A few minutes later, Big Johnson returned, having assessed the damage.

“Gotta run to Home Depot,” he said while pulling up his jeans and reaching for a T-shirt on the floor. “The heat from yesterday melted a couple of the connectors to the irrigation system.” He leaned down, kissed me on the cheek, and gave Ron Howard a tummy rub.

“You two snuggle up. And snooze till I get back.” He put his wallet in his back pocket and slid his feet into his loafers. “You have a big day ahead. I’ll be back with a latte for you.”

And then Big Johnson was out the door again.

Dad and Stepmother #1's Wedding

WHEN I WAS twelve and my sister was five, my grandparents' pastor set up my father on a blind date.

The man who baptized me, and who my grandparents believed walked on water, also dabbled in the matchmaking business. And with my father solo parenting, there wasn't much time for him to date.

Dad started spending time with his "new friend." Being a UNC alumnus who still loved attending games, he'd drive to Chapel Hill every weekend and take her to a UNC football game, leaving my sister and me to spend time with my grandparents.

They dated through the entire Tar Heel football season, but its end brought their Saturday afternoon dates to a close.

So instead of attending another football game, Dad invited my sister and me to his new friend's apartment, where we were introduced to her sullen eight-year-old son, who, when he wasn't being rude, ignored us while flaring his nostrils and baring his teeth.

The three of us followed Dad's new friend into her son's large bedroom, occupied by a twin bed, a small wooden desk, and a tiny table for playing games, where I took a seat. The table and chairs were built for five-year-olds. My butt hung over the sides. I wasn't sure where to put my long legs and arms.

"So, we've gathered you all together to let you know we're getting married," Dad announced.

The air hung heavy as if smog had filled the room. I felt dizzy and like the walls were closing in. Forced smiles plastered Dad's and his bride-to-be's faces. What? They'd just met. I'd just met her. What was her kid's name, again? Numbness seized my body. My jaw locked from clenching to hold it all in. Nausea overwhelmed me before I checked out. Left my body, drowning in feelings I couldn't process, smothered with so much confusion and hurt. Not understanding any of this.

They married the day before Valentine's Day. My sister, my new stepbrother, and I attended the wedding in the bride's parents' townhouse, officiated by their matchmaking pastor.

A month later, I turned thirteen and was instructed to call this woman "Mom."

Eight years later, she divorced my dad.

Dad and Stepmother #2's Wedding

A LONG-DISTANCE phone call from Windsor, England, to LA.

"Hi, Daddy. How are you?"

"Well, I have some news. I got married again yesterday."

"But I was hoping to meet her. I wanted to fly over and attend your wedding."

"Yeah, me too. Oh well."

Fifteen years later, she divorced my dad.

A Conversation with My Dad

"DADDY, WHAT DID you learn from each of your marriages?"

He sighed a deep sigh, allowing his shoulders to drop as he stared off into the distance before answering.

"From your mother, I learned you can't make someone love you. From marriage number two, I learned you can't make a relationship work if the other person doesn't want it. And wife number three taught me the water must be boiling when it hits the tea bag. Then steep for exactly three minutes to make the perfect cup of tea."

The Dynamic Duo

EVERYONE WANTS TO know how my father got two girlfriends.

Daddy's best friend in high school was married to Thelma for forty-five years.

Daddy's best friend in college was married to Louise for forty-two years.

When my parents were married to each other, all six of them hung out, went to parties, and played tennis, but then we moved to Massachusetts. Dad didn't return to Chapel Hill until after he married his third wife.

Then wife #3 (stepmother #2, who was Dad's boss's secretary when he worked in Windsor, England, for five years) up and left him.

Louise lost her husband, making her a widow. So she began to check in on Dad.

Then Thelma's husband died, so Dad checked in on Thelma.

The next thing we knew, Louise was traveling to Egypt with Daddy, then Thelma was cruising the Med with him.

When I asked one of them if she wanted to marry my father, she said, "God, no! I was married for too many years, looking after a man. I'm done with that." The other one felt the same way, my father being more than she wanted to deal with. I mean, he was divorced three times over.

He once told me, "I never could figure out that whole marriage thing." Which made dating the dynamic duo the perfect solution for the trio.

When I began addressing invites to my wedding, I picked up the phone and said, "Daddy, I like Louise and Thelma. I'm not sure who I should send the invite to."

"Honey, you send them both an invite and let me worry about the rest."

The next thing I knew, the dynamic duo both RSVP'd and ended up sharing a hotel room, leaving my father solo in his own room.

I'm not sure what to make of any of this other than I'm really glad they both wanted to attend.

Checking It Twice

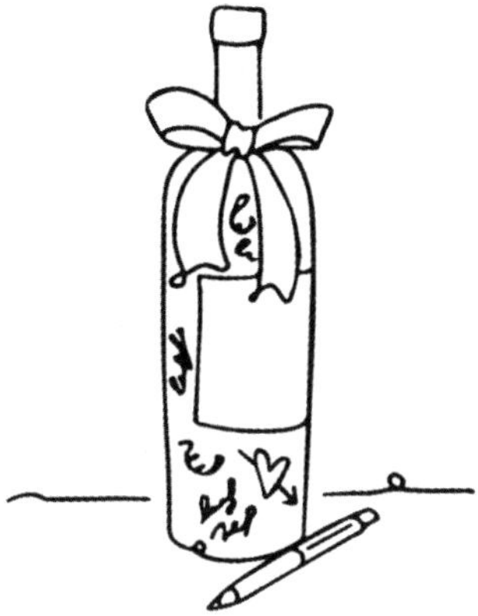

AFTER BIG JOHNSON returned with my latte, I lay in bed with Ron Howard, going over my to-do list.

The Big Johnson Wedding To-Do List

1. ~~**Something old:** engagement ring~~
2. ~~**Something new:** wedding dress~~
3. ~~**Something borrowed:** diamond stud earrings from Frankie~~
4. ~~**Something blue:** fog-blue glitter shoes~~
5. ~~Invitation list~~
6. ~~Assemble invitations~~
7. ~~Mail invitations~~
8. ~~Personalize wineglass souvenirs for guests~~

9. ~~Order cathedral-length veil~~
10. ~~Bow tie for Ron Howard~~
11. ~~Dresses and shoes for the girls~~
12. ~~Suit and tie for Big Johnson~~
13. ~~Rent folding chairs for ceremony only~~
14. ~~Rent bar-height tables and chairs~~
15. ~~Rent table linens, cloth napkins, drinking glasses, plates, and utensils~~
16. ~~Finalize fancy finger food menu~~
17. ~~Finalize rehearsal dinner menu with Frankie~~
18. ~~Purchase individual bubble blowers for guests to use for end of ceremony~~
19. Place basket of individual bubble blowers at sign-in table for guests
20. Stock all four bathrooms with towels, soap, toilet paper, flowers, and tea lights
21. Turn on tea lights and place around vineyard
22. ~~Book valet parking~~
23. Label magnum wine bottle to use as guest sign-in
24. Table for guests to sign wine bottle
25. Magic marker to sign wine bottle
26. ~~Purchase one thousand individual tea lights to decorate vineyard~~
27. ~~Cake~~
28. ~~Cake topper~~
29. ~~Wine and champagne~~
30. ~~DJ~~
31. ~~Orchids for the tables~~
32. ~~Bouquet for me and the girls; boutonniere for Big Johnson and Dad~~
33. Pick up flowers
34. ~~Hire photographer~~
35. ~~Make playlist for ceremony and party~~

36. String white lights on both balcony railings, top of pergola, and legs of pergola
37. ~~Book hotels for guests~~
38. ~~Check RSVP list~~
39. ~~Double-check RSVP list~~
40. ~~Finalize guest list~~

Once I'd finished my latte, I had the energy to start my day with a walk around the vineyard reviewing where the rentals would go when they arrived that morning.

Stepdaddy Mac

I MET HIM poolside when I was fourteen while vacationing with my mom in Miami.

He arrived late morning in a bathing suit topped with a white button-down, black business socks, and dress shoes, having flown in the night before from business in Bolivia, carrying a couple packs of Johnny Player Specials with a towel over his shoulder. Sporting gold aviators that were all the rage in the '70s, he smiled a happy grin as he stuck his hand out and said, "Hi, you must be Lisa. I'm Mac."

I stared at his black socks and dress shoes while he chuckled. "If I'd known I was going to meet you for the first time, I'd have dressed more appropriately. But when your mom said you were here, I jumped at the chance to introduce myself, so can you forgive the socks for now?"

After he lit a cigarette, he asked me how my visit was going. Then he told me about his business trip to Bolivia, explaining that his breathing problems were because of its high elevation while he chain-smoked. We stayed up all night playing "Name That Tune," listening to an oldies radio station while he drank Jack Daniel's. Mac made me laugh and he was fun, something my dad had not been since he'd married again.

The next summer I turned fifteen. Mac and my mother were living together in Chicago, and I went for my summer visit. According to my parents' divorce settlement, my sister and I were allowed to visit my mother for two weeks every summer, which my father obliged begrudgingly. Mac took us to the top of the Sears building for lunch, and while we were looking out at the vast view, he asked me if he could marry my mother.

"Yes, I'd love that," I said, so happy for her.

I could tell Mac adored my mother, and there was always a party going on when he was around.

My summer visit ended the next day when I returned to Dad and my stepmom just in time for the birth of my half brother.

♡

Mac worked as a geologist in the oil business, which made him the most well-traveled person I had met at the time. He'd lived in Iran, Singapore, and Italy before he met my mom. He was the bossman they sent to set up new oil sites, and he'd just been offered another transfer: Islamabad, Pakistan. His boss informed him, "You can go married or single, but you cannot go to a Muslim country living with a woman."

Just like my mom's dad, who'd been told he wouldn't make partner in his law firm if he didn't marry the mother of his children, marriage boiled down to a business arrangement.

Knowing my mother didn't want to get married again, Mac bought her a round-trip ticket back to the States, promising her if she wasn't happy, she could come back and file for divorce.

They married at City Hall in Chicago. Just the two of them.

Mom wore lavender jeans with a purple floral button-down silk top that she shopped from her closet. And since they had to be in Islamabad in two weeks, they packed up their apartment and moved overseas without a honeymoon.

Stepdaddy Mac's Former Wives

MAC HAD BEEN married twice before, just like my maternal grandfather.

Born and raised in Texas, a graduate of Rice College, he became a geologist for Amoco Standard Oil. On his first posting in Iran, he met Jalet, born in Tehran and schooled in England. She'd returned home because, according to Mac, "Tehran was a happening place in the early sixties." In order to marry Jalet, Mac had to convert to Islam. Being a no-nonsense atheist, he did it without much thought, taking the name Muhammad. They were married for one year.

Jalet later moved to London, where Mac and my mother lived after a few other postings. Jalet and my mother became great friends. The two women would spend hours together on the phone and meeting for tea around town. When all three of them were in their seventies, Jalet even visited my mother and Mac in the States for a week.

Jalet never remarried.

Mac met his second wife, who had also been previously married, on a bus in Manhattan. Two weeks later, Mac was transferred to Rome, so he proposed and they were married before they left. They had one son together, my supersweet stepbrother.

My mother was Mac's third and last wife.

Stepdaddy Mac's Advice

ONE DAY, WHILE Mac's son was living in Thailand, he called his dad. He was going through a breakup with a girlfriend and looking for some comfort and camaraderie. As his son shared his loss with his father, Mac left him with this thought.

"You can fall in love with anyone, but living with them is the hard part."

Stepmother #1's First Marriage

STEPMOTHER #1'S FIRST husband worked at a welcome center.

They had a son.

One day, her husband robbed the welcome center where he worked.

Instead of being sent to prison, he was admitted to a psychiatric hospital, freeing her to meet my father at a later date.

Stepmother #2's First Marriage

STEPMOTHER #2'S FIRST husband worked as a vet in Windsor, England.

They had three sons: Henry, Edward, and George.

She was English.

She was also vegetarian. Dad, a carnivore.

They drank wine together. Like, a whole lot of wine.

Traveled all over the world together.

She even got her college degree while she was his wife.

Fifteen years into marriage to my dad, she up and left, moving back to England, having won the title "Most years married to my dad."

She also became the only wife to collect alimony, and those checks kept coming until the day Dad died.

Third Time's the Charm

AS I TAKE a moment to reflect on my family lineage, this is what I've uncovered.

My maternal grandfather was married three times.

My father was married three times.

My stepfather was married three times.

And I will be Big Johnson's third time.

Obviously, third time's the charm.

Big Johnson and Tammy #1's Marriage

BIG JOHNSON MET Tammy #1 in high school.

She was the cheerleader who wouldn't give him the time of day.

Big Johnson graduated from college and, after obtaining his law degree, entered the navy, where he became JAG Johnson. JAG for judge advocate general. The navy's lawyer.

When JAG Johnson returned home, he turned Tammy's head.

JAG Johnson couldn't believe Tammy finally cheered for him, so he asked her to marry him.

By the time the honeymoon was over, Tammy #1 no longer cheered. She cried every day. Big Johnson knew the marriage was over, and they divorced within the year.

Big Johnson and Tammy #2's Marriage

BIG JOHNSON AND Tammy #2 met at the US attorney's office.

They loved to eat good food and drink fancy wines.

They had two beautiful girls together.

Ten years later, they divorced.

It was a good marriage while it lasted . . .

Big Johnson's Trying Something New

LIKE MY GRANDFATHER, father, and stepfather, Big Johnson had two previous wives.

They were both named Tammy.

So at least he's changing it up this time.

The Wedding Crasher

AFTER THE RENTALS arrived, I took stock in our four bathrooms: paper hand towels, two-ply toilet paper, single white rosebud vases. Loud banging came from the front door, followed by the doorbell looping—*ding-dong ding-dong ding-dong*—as if it were stuck. My housekeeper, busy cleaning up the remnants of last night's rehearsal dinner, stopped what she was doing and answered the door.

"Where is he?" an unfamiliar voice shouted in the high-ceilinged entryway, carrying throughout the house. I too stopped in the middle of what I was doing: meticulously hanging a new roll of toilet paper so that the paper dispensed from the front. Everyone knows it's over, not under.

"You looking for Mr. Big Johnson?"

"Yes. Where is he?" she demanded.

"I'll take you to him. He's out back in the vineyard."

I walked over to the large window above the jacuzzi in the primary bath and looked out at where the two stood below. She was dressed in tight green yoga pants and a Kenny G T-shirt, and stood with her hands on her hips.

I'd never seen this woman before. Who was she? Showing up the morning of our wedding? Demanding to see my husband-to-be?

"You're really going through with it?" mystery woman asked.

"Jane! What are you doing here?" Big Johnson's face scrunched up with a frown, looking as if a skunk had just expressed himself.

Big Johnson's previous girlfriend was named Jane. He'd spoken of her only briefly, and I'd seen a couple photos, but never live in person. She was skinnier in person.

"You and me. We were supposed to get married," she pleaded, her voice cracking.

He shook his head, setting down his recent Home Depot purchases. "What are you doing here and why would you think that?"

"Because we spent six years together."

He reached for his Diet Pepsi and took a long swig before he spoke again. "But I never asked you. Six years on and off was more than enough time to realize we were never going to work out."

She leaned in, roped her arms around his neck like a lasso, and tried to kiss him.

When he pushed her away, she started down the driveway back to her car.

"She makes me really, really happy!" he called after her.

My heart cracked open as I watched her leave. Love hurts when it's not reciprocated. I'd been there. Had my own heart broken before. I also saw with my own two eyes that Big Johnson chose me again in that moment. I didn't know I could love him any more.

It's Not Lost on Me

BIG JOHNSON HAS two daughters, just like Dad.

Dad was an officer in the navy and wanted to be a lawyer but dropped out of law school.

Big Johnson became a JAG, then a federal prosecutor for the United States Organized Crime Strike Force, and ultimately opened his own law practice.

They both drink wine, lots of wine. Dad out of a box. Big Johnson out of expensive bottles.

Both are Southerners.

Both love to travel anywhere.

It's not lost on me.

A Conversation with My Mother

"DO YOU KNOW what Johnson means in England?" she asked.

"Penis? Dick?"

"Yes," she whispered, her eyebrows arched so high they hid behind her hairline.

"It means the same thing here in the States, Mom."

The Colonel and Shirley Johnson (the Future In-Laws)

JOHNNY MET SHIRLEY at a VFW (Veterans of Foreign Wars) Valentine's dance.

"The Colonel," as Johnny was more affectionately called by his family, served in the marines for forty years. Saw World War II, Korea, and Vietnam. Since he spent his early years in Asia, he was "engaged" six times, gifting each woman a strand of pearls. Pearls were all the rage for military officers to give their girls as a symbol of commitment, and Johnny had sprung for six before Shirley.

She was a surgical nurse.

They danced together every night and were in love.

They were married for sixty-two years until Shirley died.

Johnny died nine months later.

The Colonel and Shirley's RSVP

BY THE TIME the big day arrived, Shirley and Johnny were unable to travel across the country to Big Johnson Winery, so I made the photographers promise to capture every guest who attended so we'd be able to share them with the Johnsons.

When I received our final photos and matched them to the guest list, I saw I had no documentation of half the attendees.

A False Start

TECHNICALLY I HAD been "in" weddings since before I was born. When I was thirteen, I was a bridesmaid for my father's second marriage. And then in my early twenties, a bridesmaid for my college roommate, Bobbie. Not her first wedding.

I had only been privy to bits and pieces of her first wedding since it happened before we became friends. Rumor had it, she was supposed to get married in a big church wedding in downtown Charleston on Church Street. Hundreds of people came, including Mayor Riley.

Lots of dough was spent on the dress, flowers, and food.

And then . . .

The groom never showed.

So instead of the honeymoon suite on the beach in Bali, Bobbie checked into a high-end spa, where she spent two months in round-the-clock therapy.

A few years later, we were roommates in college, and on a random evening we found ourselves enjoying a pitcher of beer during happy hour in a bar called Daddy's Money in our tiny college town of Rock Hill, South Carolina.

Other than a few people at the bar, the place was deserted. Cigarette stench swirled with last night's spilled beer that stuck to the bottom of my Tretorn tennis shoes. A long-haired guitar player sang sad Loggins and Messina songs. After a full day of student teaching, Bobbie was bitching about her fourth-grade music students' lack of rhythm on the autoharp when she glanced over at the bar and squinted—hard.

Then she stared, even harder, and said, "What's that mother-fucker doing here?"

"Who?"

"Greg!"

"Greg?" I asked, whipping my head around to see who she was referring to.

"The son of a bitch who stood me up at the altar."

"Wait! What?"

"What's he doing here?" she cried. "In Rock Hill?"

"He's here? Where?"

"That's him." Bobbie threw back her beer, slamming the empty glass on the marred wooden table.

"Which one?"

"Brown hair, black leather jacket, standing at the bar drinking Coors."

I scanned the bar until I found him—tall, dark curly hair, snug jeans that showed off his fit body, and well-worn black cowboy boots. He held himself with the confidence of Superman. A cape and tights would have completed the look.

"I'm gonna go ask that cocksucker where he's been," Bobbie said as she kicked the chair out from beneath her and headed toward the bar while "Angry Eyes" pumped through the small amp by the bar.

Glued to my chair, I watched Bobbie walk with purpose to the bar, her back to me.

She tapped Greg on the shoulder.

He turned around.

His face transformed from a deep ruffled brow to wide-eyed to a slack jaw large enough to park a school bus.

Bobbie's blond curls jiggled from the back of her head.

His mouth moved while he shook his head.

I reached for the pitcher and refilled both of our glasses, never taking my eyes off of them.

He spoke again.

Then she turned around and stomped back to our table, fireworks exploding with each step she took before she sat down again.

"Well?" I asked.

"Pussy. Said he woke up that day and didn't want to get married so he got in his truck and drove to Florida, where he's been for the past two years." She took a long swig from her glass and exhaled as if she had been holding her breath. "Says he had no idea I was going to school here. I should have dumped his beer on his head."

Her jaw muscles clenched while she glared at his back. "Seriously? That's all he's got?" she asked.

Silence fell between us while "Fire and Rain" wailed from the solo guitar player.

Then Bobbie kicked the leg of the chair sitting between us, taking it down for the count.

We ordered another pitcher to drown her tears and drank ourselves silly. Bobbie called in sick the next day, and we both threw up for the next two.

♡

Two years later, Bobbie met Dean. He proposed, and she decided to wed at another downtown Charleston church. Gotta hand it to her for showing up again.

I arrived in my yellow taffeta bridesmaid dress on a sunny Saturday morning, the humidity mild while puffy clouds moved through the Carolina blue sky. Sailboats tacked across the Charleston Harbor. It was indeed a beautiful day.

Just inside the front door of the church, Bobbie paced back and forth in a long, lacy white dress, wearing out the carpet below. I tried to keep up, holding her white rose and lily bouquet while organ music bellowed out of the sanctuary and through the entrance. It was time.

I held Bobbie's hand. "You don't have to do this," I said, pleading into her beautiful soft aquamarine eyes. "We can run away, right now. My dad's car is parked across the street."

Bobbie fidgeted with the lace on the wrist of the sleeve and stared into my eyes as she exhaled. She pursed her lips before her mouth moved but nothing came out. I could sense her hesitation. The air became weighty.

This time it was her turn to run if she wasn't ready, and it was okay if she wasn't. She was far too young, and I didn't know of any marriages that had worked out. I was ready to aid and abet her to walk away, run away, drive away, if she wanted to bail.

She shook her head, her blond curls emphasizing her decision bouncing side to side.

I hugged her, took my place in line, and walked the commitment shuffle toward the altar in my floor-length yellow dress that I never wore again.

Ten years later, Bobbie and Dean divorced.

A Holdup

STILL REELING FROM Big Johnson's revelation about the signatures, I gazed into the bathroom mirror while watching Frankie tighten my halter straps by attaching a safety pin securely behind my neck, making them snug.

This is the moment where I usually take the bride aside and tell her, "It's not too late. Make a run for it now." Staring at myself in a wedding dress with a wedding band on my finger that officially meant nothing. Maybe God was telling me something like, "I just opened a window for you! You're not up to be part of the institution. Escape this entrapment. The papers aren't signed. You're still single."

“Here, that should hold those suckers up,” Frankie said just before we both looked into the bathroom mirror and laughed at the ridiculousness of the moment.

I needed to find the keys to my car. Where did I leave them?

“Come on, we’ve got guests to entertain,” she said as she opened the bathroom door.

The scent of freshly baked bread wafted through the open kitchen. An orchestra of pots and pans clanged while the caterers moved about preparing the finger food menu. “The Game of Love” blared through the speakers as I opened the door onto the main patio where “the ceremony” had just taken place. Big Johnson’s entire office staff stood around one of the bar tables noshing on the hot upside-down mushroom tarts. The secretary from his office asked, “How does it feel to be Mrs. Johnson?”

Really, now? Not now! I have no idea.

“Excuse me, I need to find the keys to my car. Where did I leave them?” I grabbed a shrimp skewer and shoved it into my mouth as I walked away.

I’d opted for fancy finger foods, like lamb lollipops and skewered shrimp with tiny kabobs, all served on sticks so if you didn’t like who you were talking to, you could easily walk away with your dinner in your hand. No one would get stuck sitting next to anyone they didn’t want to talk to at my wedding. I’d set it up this way for many reasons, but mostly to protect my parents from running into each other.

With a magnum of Silver Oak on his shoulder, Big Johnson filled another guest’s glass.

“Did you find the marriage certificate?” I asked.

“It’s safe, in a folder where I put it.”

“What do we do now?” I fiddled with the new safety pin holding up the halter, wondering if it was strong enough or going to come undone and stick me in the neck before it fell down, leaving me full-frontal exposed.

"Don't worry. I'll take care of it, honey." He landed a quick kiss on my lips before he turned to fill someone else's glass and moved through our celebratory friends and family.

I needed a drink.

Flower Power

WHILE SITTING AT one of the high-top tables in the middle of the patio, giving my feet a rest from all the standing and having just freed myself from the walking cast, I inspected the table decorations I'd put together. White linen tablecloths with matching cloth napkins, a mirrored place mat in the center. On top of the mirror, a single white tea light candle and a white orchid in a small white pot in the center. Simple and elegant, with a little Hollywood glam.

There's an old *Dennis the Menace* comic where he's coming out of the florist with his father, who's holding a bouquet of flowers. Dennis looks up at his dad and asks, "Why buy her flowers? She could eat candy?"

I agree with Dennis. Candy is the best way to my heart. Not chocolate. Sugar. Lots of sugar. My favorites: Hot Tamales and Smarties. Bring on the sugar.

I like flowers, just not fresh-cut flowers every week. They're a poor investment. They die before you have time to fully enjoy them. And let's face it: From the moment you cut that blossom, you've contributed to its death.

Big Johnson loves cut flowers, and he loves buying them for me. Red gladiolas are his favorite. He's crazy about the orange-red ones, my least favorite color. But giving me flowers makes him happy, and since I've accepted that, I'm a lot happier and I can buy my own candy.

Frankie's Glam Gram and Hurricane Husband

FEELING UNDERDRESSED IN my pajamas, I sat around the small breakfast table in the middle of the kitchen with Frankie's eighty-five-year-old grandma. Unlike me, Grandma dressed for breakfast. She was a tiny woman with long giraffe-like gams covered in pale lemon polyester pants topped with a vibrant Versace blouse. Like a model on a runway, she paraded around in five-inch stilettos with a full face of makeup. Her platinum blond hair coiffed as if she'd just walked out of the beauty parlor, which in Florida with 100 percent humidity is quite the magic trick. An array of gold bangles jangled from each arm while Obsession by Calvin Klein swirled around the room. Fire-engine red her color choice on her immaculate manicured hands.

Right after I turned thirty, Frankie, my new best friend who was a few years younger than me, asked me to be her maid of honor. To save money for the wedding, she put me up in her parents' house next door to her grandma.

With Hurricane Edna heading toward Fort Lauderdale and Frankie's dream wedding on a boat now canceled, the wedding was happening at a Ramada Inn, leaving me home alone with Glam Gram, who wore stilettos to breakfast.

"Are you married?" Glam Gram clanged the side of the ceramic mug, stirring Sweet'N Low into her black coffee while a sweet and tart smell hung from the empty pink sweetener packet.

"No, not yet." Here it was. The same question old people ask me. I buttered my bagel.

Taking a slight pause before she spoke next, Glam Gram inhaled. "Well . . . what are you doing about it?" Her brow furrowed. A look of urgency appeared as she leaned forward and pursed her lips.

Putting down my knife, I looked at her. *Doing? What? Why?* Hadn't my parents told me I couldn't get married until after thirty? I could barely keep my head above water—working, paying rent, while having fun and being young. "Uh, hanging out with Frankie? She's so much fun."

"Yes, but are you going to synagogue?"

"I'm not Jewish."

"Are you a member of any clubs?"

"You mean as in yacht or country?"

"Yes."

"Uh . . . no."

Glam Gram sipped her coffee. Her shoulders fell as she exhaled with exasperation. "Are you asking friends to set you up?"

"Not really." The warm and cozy kitchen began to feel like a police interrogation room. I scanned the room looking for the closest exit.

"Are you going to dances?"

I looked at her and smiled. "I like to dance." My head nodded up and down like a bobblehead. Was this what she wanted to hear?

Taking a sip of coffee, she looked deep into my eyes. "May I ask how old you are, dear?"

"Thirty-one?" That's almost thirty. Still in the have-fun zone.

Ice cubes dropped into the freezer while the refrigerator hummed.

Glam Gram's smile fell into a frown followed by a deep and sorrowful sigh. "Oh." She stared down into her empty coffee mug for a moment. A long moment. As if she were grasping for something, anything to say now that she knew my truth. I looked down at the huge diamond solitaire on her left ring finger. Nothing more could be done. My date had expired. Glam Gram was sure I'd never wear one of those.

She dropped her perfectly coiffed platinum blond head, scooted her chair back from the table, placed her dirty mug in the sink, and walked back to her room, the *clickety-clack* of her high heels bouncing off the hallway, trailing until she closed the bedroom door behind her.

Frankie's marriage, like Hurricane Edna, didn't last long but was turbulent while it happened. But let's face it, the signs were there on her wedding day, and I did say what I always say to my soon-to-be-married friends before they walk down the aisle: "It's not too late. You don't have to do this. We can run." And believe me when I tell you her ceremony was a dismal affair in that conference room at the Ramada Inn with fake flowers, gray carpeting, and fluorescent lighting.

I wanted to run—and I wasn't the one getting married.

"The trouble with some women is that they get all excited about nothing—and then marry him."

—Cher

Hunk of Burning Love

RIGHT AFTER I moved to Los Angeles, I attended an elopement. The bride and groom rented a stretch limo and drove three witnesses to Vegas for the weekend: the bride's best friend, Joey; the groom's best friend, Howie; and me. I'd known the couple for a few weeks.

On Friday afternoon after work, our chauffeur, George, arrived in a long black stretch limo. All five of us piled into the back. Notorious bumper-to-bumper LA traffic was no longer our concern. Behind George's tinted glass, the rehearsal party had commenced. Champagne corks flew, joints were passed, and acid was dropped while cigarette ashes dusted the carpeted floor below. We thought we were rock stars, and we'd come prepared. Not only with lots of mood-altering substances, but also four 35 mm cameras, one Bell & Howell 8, along with a Nikon Super 8, with everyone's favorite . . . the Bolex 16 mm. It was 1993, long before the days of the cell phone, and since all five of us worked in the film business, it was all about documenting this monumental moment.

Once we hit the desert, a good four hours into our "trip," we'd gone to far-out places. George pulled off to the side of the road, turning off his engine and lights. Not a streetlamp or car in sight. In total darkness and silence, we gazed up at the stars above. So many stars—sparkling, twinkling, and shining. None of us had ever seen such a sky like that at night. Shooting stars and constellations with galaxies light-years away. I felt small, so small among the vastness of the sky that night. Discussions of alien landings and abductions occupied our minds. Would we go willingly and be experimented on? I shivered. Perhaps it was the cool breeze of the desert night, the talk of UFOs, or maybe another wave of the acid rolling in, but I took refuge back in the limo and dined on a tin of Pringles.

George dropped us off at the Bellagio sometime around 11 p.m. We spent the rest of the evening tripping up and down the Strip, pulling slot machines along the way.

The next morning at the breakfast buffet, the bride taught me how to play keno. We filled out our betting slips and handed them to our waitress while we drank pots of coffee to sober up, waiting for our winning numbers to be displayed. Keno was not our game.

After breakfast, the bride and groom set off for the Clark County office to get their license. I took this as an opportunity to grab a midmorning nap. Once our to-be-wedded friends returned to the hotel, we dressed in fancy clothes, iced five bottles of Dom Pérignon, and loaded all the cameras with film while George drove us to the Graceland Wedding Chapel.

The three o'clock ceremony had been purchased along with the "Can't Help Falling in Love with You" package. It included a fresh bouquet for the bride, a boutonniere for the groom, three Elvis songs of their choice, and special Elvis vows performed by "Elvis" himself. All for three hundred and fifty dollars. Elvis was also available to walk the bride down the aisle if needed for "no additional fee."

The three of us surrounded the couple as they exchanged simple gold bands, the groom's engraved "To My Hunk a Hunk of Burning Love," while Elvis sang "Love Me Tender." The groom's chest puffed out with pride as he gazed into his radiant bride's brown eyes, which had been refreshed with Visine just moments before the ceremony began.

The reception was held at the renowned Golden Steer, where the real Elvis dined in his day. We celebrated at the Frank Sinatra table and feasted on lobster, rib eyes, twice-baked potatoes, and macaroni and cheese. For dessert, cherries jubilee flambéed tableside before we caught the hot new show in Vegas, something called Cirque du Soleil's *Nouvelle Expérience*, under a tent behind the Mirage Hotel.

After we slept in and had a late checkout, George returned us to LA on Sunday evening.

A few years later, our careers would cause us to drift apart.

Then, on New Year's Eve 1999, while strolling down Cheyne Walk toward the River Thames for the midnight millennium firework celebration in London, who did I bump into? None other than the Hunk of Burning Love and his bride with their five-year-old son.

We talked about getting together when we were back in LA, but it never happened.

Ten years later, they divorced.

Stuffed

I MET ANDI while editing my first Toyota commercial.

A copywriter for a huge advertising agency, Andi was one of a handful of women I ever worked with in a very male business. Sarcastic with a great sense of humor, she saw the world similar to me, only darker, and since we were the only two women in the room, we bonded the moment we met.

Andi had been with her partner, Talulah, going on six years, and in 2008, a quick window opened where gay marriage became legal in California. So Talulah proposed. They had a small wedding in their big, beautiful beach home. Talulah invited her ex-husband and sat him next to me hoping to set us up, but it went no further than their reception dinner.

Andi's conservative mother, Suzy, raised in Mobile, Alabama, sat on my other side. Suzy was a petite woman with bright blue eyes, her skin wrinkly from days gardening in the hot sun growing tomatoes, cucumbers, and squash.

After we watched Andi and Talulah cut their cake, while waiting for our slice, Suzy turned to me and said, "I've never understood this whole gay thing, but I'm really glad my daughter's so happy." She smiled and turned back to watch Andi feed Talulah cake.

Before the honeymoon was even over, Andi moved out and into a furnished rental. Their relationship had always been volatile as they were both high-powered professional women. When I drove to visit Andi in her new digs, I found my friend in a deep depression, surrounded by death. Her rental was fully furnished, all right—taxidermy furnished.

A dead armadillo hung above the sofa, while a stiff baby bear lay on its back, all four paws used to hold the glass top for the coffee table. Chairs for the dining room were made from cow horns. Small antlers lined an entire wall—for coats and hats. Badgers and deer and wolves staged everywhere. Andi shuffled around her temporary home, oblivious to the extermination and termination surrounding her.

"You're coming to live with me until you get your shit together," I said while I packed up her stuff.

♡

Andi moved into my two-bedroom, two-bath townhouse that very day. Like the odd couple, she was Oscar Madison to my Felix Unger.

On weekends, she stayed up all night drinking my entire wine collection and slept until noon while obsessing over how to serve Talulah divorce papers first. Andi's lawyer informed her that it was to her advantage to be the first to serve papers because it would allow her to control the timeline of the process, set the narrative early on, and secure temporary orders like asset protection before Talulah had a chance to file her response, giving her a slight edge in the legal proceedings.

Andi took measures to make sure she didn't get served first. She began wearing disguises. A long brunette wig, a baseball cap, and sunglasses. Parked her Toyota Camry blocks from my condo, retrieving it only through alleyways, dodging public places to avoid any possible person with an envelope. It was a crazy way to live.

Eventually, Andi won the serve and she returned to dressing like herself. Six months later, she moved into her own place—with a live dog she rescued from the pound.

The Great Escape

SOMETIME AROUND NOON on our wedding day, our three-tiered red velvet cake with buttercream frosting arrived via Doan's Bakery. Doan's Bakery is world famous for their white chocolate coconut cake that Tom Cruise sends out to hundreds of his friends every Christmas. It's not what I choose when I go there. I got fat off of their cinnamon rolls. They are the size of a Frisbee, as heavy as a brick, and the most delicious sweet I've ever had.

My loyalty to this place, not far from the vineyard, had not wavered, so the cake had been ordered early on. The delivery guy walked through the front door, both hands occupied and therefore unable to close the door behind him. As soon as he placed the cake on the dining room table, Paws, the bigger and more adventurous of Big Johnson's feline tabby twins, took the opportunity to break free from all the pre-wedding chaos and make a run for it—out the front door, down the concrete steps, through the terraced vines, where he crossed the road and climbed up a very tall tree.

Our neighbor Freddie was walking his dog, Buddy—the largest bloodhound I'd ever seen. Buddy stopped to bark at Paws, who scampered even higher up the tree. Big Johnson ran out and ordered Paws to climb down the tree.

Paws responded by climbing farther up until he reached another limb, sat in the crux of it, and stared down.

Ron Howard and I walked down to take a look up at Paws. I'd never actually encountered a cat up a tree before. Only seen them do it in the movies. Cats were and still are a mystery to me.

Our housekeeper came running down the hill with a box of Meow Mix and handed it to Big Johnson. The big bloodhound moved on and began trekking up the much-loved hiking trail behind the vineyard.

"Paws, get down from there, right now," Big Johnson demanded.

Paws meowed and sauntered farther out on the limb.

Other neighbors walked by on their way to the trail behind the vineyard, stopping to gawk at Paws's dilemma, then hurried up the dirt hill.

Big Johnson started to shake the box of Meow Mix, which normally got Paws running for a bowl full of the artificially colored processed chemical cookies, but this time it had no effect.

After forty-five minutes of watching Big Johnson shake the treat box like a maraca in a Caribbean band while rapping for him to come down from the tree, while hikers passed by offering no help, I picked up Ron Howard and hugged him for some inspiration. Then I proposed another option.

"Shall I call the fire department?" I'd only ever seen firemen get cats out of trees on TV, as it was clear thirty minutes ago that the shaking was futile.

"They don't rescue cats anymore." Big Johnson shook the box again. "They're too busy rescuing people. Stay here and watch him. I'm gonna get a ladder."

I shook the box and sang a tune that popped to mind: "What's new pussycat? Whoa, whoa, whoa! What's new pussycat? Whoa, whoa, whoa, whoa."

Paws was not impressed by my Tom Jones rendition and tried to scurry up to an even higher limb, but he was as high as his little body could go. Ron Howard seemed to enjoy my singing. But he always did.

Big Johnson arrived with his extension ladder, extending it to full length, leaned it against the tree, and climbed to the top rung. A neighbor had stopped and offered to hold the base of the ladder. I watched as he climbed each rung, my heart racing as I envisioned a misstep followed by a fall just a few hours before our wedding. I'd just stepped out of my cast yesterday, and he'd be the one wearing one at the ceremony.

Paws looked down, still a good three feet out of Big Johnson's reach.

Back on the ground, Big Johnson gave the box another shake and said, "Paws, I got a wedding to go to." He looked at the box, then up to Paws, and shook his head.

Freddie, now returning from his hike with Buddy, looked up and said, "Wow! How long has he been up there?"

"Too long," Big Johnson said, followed by a sigh. But then his face brightened and he turned back to Freddie. "Wait! I have an idea! And I need your help."

In a flash, Big Johnson returned in Bubba, his ten-year-old Toyota Tundra.

"I'm gonna need you to hold the ladder from the bed of the truck," Big Johnson informed our wide-eyed neighbor. "That should boost me the distance I need to reach him."

Big Johnson maneuvered the truck next to the tree so he could prop up the ladder in it while Freddie held the bottom. Freddie was a horse jockey, so he was not only tiny but also couldn't have weighed more than one hundred pounds wet, and yet he was the one steadying all three hundred pounds of Big Johnson as he moved up the ladder to where it ended right at Paws's paws. He grabbed Paws and carried him like a football as he worked his way back down the extended ladder while Freddie did his best to keep the top-heavy ladder grounded to the truck bed.

By the time Big Johnson hit the truck bed, a crowd of people had stopped to watch the show and gave him a round of applause. Sweat dripped from his face, his T-shirt soaked. He smiled as he thanked Freddie, who shouted, "Congratulations and best wishes on your big day!," before he and Buddy began heading home.

I looked at Ron Howard and said, "I'm definitely a dog girl."

Firsts

MY FIRST MEMORIES of the opposite sex are on the playground of the University Baptist Church in Chapel Hill, North Carolina, during the recess hour of my day-care years. I'm not clear about the game, but I was chasing a boy who was running as fast and as far away from me as he could. He may even have been screaming. Or maybe that was me.

It wasn't until sixth grade when I found my first official steady, Colt Williams. He had wavy blond hair and eyes as aqua as the country club swimming pool where he entertained me. We'd sit on the edge, dangling our legs in the water while we giggled. Then we'd dine on burgers and fries while his mother played bridge with her girlfriends poolside. Colt oozed kindness and sweetness. He complimented me on my wardrobe and always had ideas on how to style my long hair. Twenty years later I found out he'd moved to the Castro in San Francisco, where he met the love of his life, Butch.

In seventh grade, Jimmy Thomas was the first boy I made out with under the bleachers at the Friday night high school football game. He had buck teeth, harnessed by braces, and brown marble eyes that were slightly crossed, with straight dark blond hair, cut like a helmet. And he was short. Think a budding John Denver minus the guitar.

Then there was Duke, the first older boy I "went with." I was an eighth grader, Duke a ninth-grade JV football player—running back. Duke lived with his grandmother, and when he called me on Saturday and Sunday mornings, I could hear Ric Flair, André the Giant, and Hulk Hogan body-slamming in the ring while his grandma shouted at the TV in the background. For Christmas, Duke bought me a Sarah Coventry pearl necklace his aunt sold at one of her home parties. I never took it off.

Then there was Jarret Baylor. We met in the ninth-grade stage band. His instrument was the trumpet, mine alto sax. We played the country club dance scene. Jarret stood tall with a silent, kind confidence that I'd never experienced before. A real gentleman. I felt safe with him. But then my dad's job transferred us to another state.

The High School Boyfriend

SOME MIGHT SAY I fell for Cooper when I tripped over a two-by-four lying on the side of the road on the very first day we moved into our house on Sidney Street in Charleston.

I turned fifteen that year. Sunnyland was a contemporary housing development still under construction. Jogging was all the rage in the '70s, so I thought I'd give it a try: take a jog around the neighborhood, something I had never done before—or since. And that's when I laid eyes on the towheaded surfer dude sliding into his candy-apple-red '77 Mustang. I stared so hard at him, I didn't see the plank in my path that took me face down in the freshly paved street, resulting in a cast all the way up to my knee. Sporting crutches was not the fashion accessory to make a cool first impression at my new school.

Luckily, the bus stopped in front of our house, so I didn't have to hobble far. Cooper's mother, in a full-length navy robe and scuff slippers, walked down her driveway every morning to retrieve the newspaper delivered at the edge of her driveway. We'd wave, smile, and exchange "Good mornings" as she picked up the day's news to savor with a cup of coffee and her first cigarette of the day. One of those mornings, Cooper came out to retrieve the paper for his mom. Seeing me on crutches, he offered to drive me to school—and that's how it started.

A relationship built on pity and proximity! But location, location, location is how most relationships start, right?

Cooper had a couple looks—jeans and a T-shirt during the week and flip-flops and surfer Birdwell Beach britches on weekends, even though we never once went to the beach. Soon after we started commuting to school together, we became an item. Every Friday night Cooper took me to our local Pizza Hut for a pepperoni and mushroom pizza with a trip to the salad bar for iceberg lettuce, cucumbers, pepperoncini, and fake bacon bits, smothered in creamy Italian dressing. Afterward, we'd drive to the airport and park. The stated purpose was to watch the planes land, but I don't recall seeing any planes through the fogged-up windows.

What I liked about Cooper was his family—his two older sisters and his mother most of all. They invited me to sit at their kitchen table when they were dining or just to sit while they smoked and chatted about anything. I was always welcomed, and I felt wanted. Cooper would fix me a glass of sweet iced tea, and I'd grab a seat next to his mom and listen to her talk about entertaining her children and grandchildren for the weekend. She loved her family and made every weekend a party for them.

So unlike my own house across the street, where I was uncomfortable in my own bedroom, much less anywhere else in my house. Kind words were foreign with a stepmother far from nurturing, unable to comfort or offer encouragement during those awkward teenage years. On the rare occasion when she did speak to me, it was to let me know a toilet needed to be scrubbed, or the table needed to be set, or the dishwasher needed to be unloaded. I dodged her the best I could.

Having to defend that I wanted to wear my hair long or why I needed a new pair of shoes was exhausting, and I sensed I wasn't important or wanted. That I didn't matter. And that I had no needs. Every day I tiptoed barefoot on shattered glass while she took inventory of all my faults. And she spotted them all.

During those years I learned to fly stealth—became invisible, slipping in, avoiding being noticed. I felt so invisible I started to believe I was.

Most nights, after everyone fell asleep, I snuck out of the house, crossed the street, and knocked on Cooper's back door, where he'd let me into his room above the garage. I'd hang out for a few hours, smoke cigarettes, and have sex while listening to Exile's "Kiss You All Over" over and over again with some Boston, Kansas, and Foreigner thrown into the mix.

Cooper was my first.

As soon as Cooper and I started to have sex, we did the responsible thing: drove to the free clinic to get the Pill. At fifteen I knew this wasn't something Dad, much less the stepmother, could or would support, so I hid the pills in a watch box in the back of my nightstand drawer where no one was supposed to be poking around except me.

But sure enough, one night my father marched into my bedroom screaming, slamming the door behind him.

"Your mother found these in your room today!" His face beet red as he handed me the white plastic pill package retrieved from the watch box.

My legs wobbled. I wanted to run, but my feet cemented to the floor. My arms went numb as my shoulders reached up to my ears as if they could stop the fury flying toward me. I squeezed my eyes tight, not wanting to see the monster in front of me.

"You are heading down a dark road!" His face now so contorted I thought he might have a stroke. I'd never ever seen him so mad.

He became so worked up that at one point he threw a wooden chair at me.

My father had always had a scary side to him, but this was rage.

When Cooper told his parents that my father found out we'd been sleeping together, they took it all in stride and loved me all the same. With Cooper having two older sisters already married, his parents had experience and just accepted it as part of growing up.

A year into our relationship, Cooper gave me a tiny chipped diamond promise ring and asked me to marry him in the back seat of his Mustang. A few weeks later, we got into an argument in his beloved car—where else? He took the ring off my finger, got out of the car, placed it under the rear tire on the driver's side, and ran over it again and again and again. I stood on the side of the abandoned road, frozen in fear, watching the tire treads back over the gravel road—back and forth, back and forth, the crunch of the gravel accompanied by the occasional spin of the tires as he whipped it from forward to reverse. Eventually, I got back in the car and he drove us the four blocks home.

I had long been aware of the way Cooper carried himself. There was an awkwardness in his body. An unease. His laugh felt forced, and there was anger buried deep down that had started to emerge more and more. I was familiar with this kind of anger from my father, but Cooper and his family had always felt more safe than home.

My senior year in high school, my dad took my stepmother on a vacation, leaving her parents to look after us. Cooper and I hit the roller-skating rink that Friday night. We skated in circles for an hour before a small kid fell in front of me. I tumbled on top of the child, and the next thing I knew I was in the skating rink office, wedged into a desk made for first graders with my arm, elbow to middle finger, held in a flimsy cardboard box after some cute guy helped me off the skating rink.

Cooper glared at the cute guy helping me up and stormed off, leaving me stranded.

The cute guy offered to take me to the emergency room to get my arm X-rayed.

The empty emergency room was oddly quiet for a Friday night. I stood in a large white room while an X-ray tech—with bloodshot hazel eyes, sporting baby-blue surgical scrubs he'd clearly outgrown, breathing onions he was still digesting—moved my arm into different positions. He did his best to try to take my mind off of the physical pain and the fact that I had been abandoned by my boyfriend at the roller rink only to be escorted by a stranger who was indeed cute, but a stranger still. As he slid the next piece of film in and rotated my elbow, he inquired, "So where do you work?," while adjusting my wrist to lie flat.

"McDonald's."

He tilted his head, double-checking his latest X-ray, and began to sing, "You deserve a break today at McDonald's," reciting the popular jingle.

The last buzzer sound went off, and the tech returned to remove the heavy leaded apron, continuing, "So get up and get away to McDonald's."

I moved into the casting room escorted by the stranger. That's when Cooper arrived swinging, looking for a fight, and that's what he got—a fistfight in the casting room with my cute stranger as I waited for the doctor to plaster my arm. Eventually, security removed them both from the room.

My stepgrandmother arrived at the hospital, baffled and confused. Once I got home, I was grounded until my father and stepmother returned from their vacation.

I dreamed of the time when I could move away . . . far away.

So when college application time came around, I applied to four in-state colleges and was accepted into all. I chose the one farthest away from home. Whatever pent-up anger, disappointment, jealousy, and hurt I carried, I'd leave it on Sidney Street along with Cooper.

The Musician

WE MET IN the back seat of a '76 lemon-yellow Pontiac LeMans on a drug run.

It was a Friday night, first semester of my freshman year at a small college in the tiny town of Rock Hill. He was an older man, a sophomore, dressed in well-worn Wranglers, a threadbare flannel shirt, and tan suede Wallabee boots. With a chestnut shag just to his shoulders, the Musician shared a smile as big as Scooby-Doo. Actually, he was probably more like Shaggy from the cartoon, only the Musician was soft-spoken and said sweet and funny things that made me giggle.

Not only did I fall for the Musician that night, but I also fell asleep in the car during the drug deal. Forty-plus years later I would learn that the Musician had also stolen a keyboard for one of his band members from a church that night. I can't verify if our drug connection was connected to the church, but I'd found out I'd not only been on an illegal pot run, I'd also aided and abetted in my sleep.

He came from a deeply religious family. His siblings all youth ministers, music directors of churches, and deacons while the Musician sang in bars, smoked pot, and drank alcohol.

One night, not long after our drug run, the Musician serenaded me outside my dorm window with the James Taylor song "Something in the Way She Moves." All the girls in my dorm hung out their windows and swooned. Our college had formerly been an all-girls school, coed for just the past ten years. Guys were still scarce, so to snag one was a real coup. And a musician as cute and talented as he was, well, it was a fucking miracle.

The Musician was kind and had serious Southern manners. Walked on the correct side of the street, opened all doors, escorted me wherever I was going, and always called when he said he would. This was not something I had experienced before. Certainly not from my family of origin. He listened to me. Held my hand. Asked me what I wanted while his kisses lit me up like Christmas lights and the sex was New Year's fireworks every time all the time. He made it all about me. My body wanted to be close to his every day all day long.

The Musician rode a bicycle around campus to get to his classes. Occasionally, I'd sit on the front bar sideways, watching the autumn leaves fall from trees above. If we walked, he carried my books. We'd make out every chance we got. I even wore his fraternity jersey.

You could find me in the audience at every performance whether he performed solo or with the band. He taught me to swing dance to beach music, making me feel like Ginger Rogers when he twirled me across the floor.

♡

My sophomore year, to help pay for college, I became a resident assistant in a female-only dorm on campus. The main part of my job was to make sure there was no trouble on my floor, like no men allowed past midnight and no drugs, but I broke all the rules. The Musician stayed over every night, and one could always find a towel under the bottom of my door to keep the pot smell from wafting down the hallway.

On Valentine's Day, the Musician arrived with a small heart-shaped box of chocolates. Inside, among the nougats and cream-filled delights, sparkled an amethyst ring, just my size. Amethyst symbolizes deep love and happiness, and that was what I felt for him.

The Musician and I were together on and off for seven years. But then one day, during a moment we were off, he took a girl away for a weekend gig in another town. When I found out, my legs gave out, and I fell onto the cold black-and-while linoleum in my kitchen, where I sobbed for three days. My heart hurt. My body ached. I had no idea loving someone could hurt so much.

I moved to North Carolina after the breakup, magically thinking he would follow me, but he didn't. It would take me years to understand that we didn't want the same thing. I thought he wanted what I wanted: to take the next step, to move to a bigger television market. A bigger music market. But he was happy right where he was. Without me.

Big Johnson Wedding Playlist

September 3, 2011

Walking down the aisle: "At Last"/Etta James
End of ceremony: "We Are Family"/Sister Sledge

1. "Celebration"/Kool & the Gang
2. "Shake Your Groove Thing"/Peaches & Herb
3. "You're the First, the Last, My Everything"/Barry White
4. "You Can't Resist It"/Lyle Lovett
5. "Summer Breeze"/The Isley Brothers

6. "September"/Earth, Wind & Fire
7. "Now That We Found Love"/Third World
8. "Amazing"/Seal
9. "Baby, Now That I've Found You"/Alison Krauss
10. "C'est Si Bon"/Eartha Kitt
11. "California Dreamin'"/Queen Latifah
12. "Cheek to Cheek"/ Ella Fitzgerald and Louis Armstrong
13. "Feeling Good"/Nina Simone
14. "Family Affair"/Steve Winwood
15. "Glad You Came"/The Wanted
16. "Higher Ground"/Stevie Wonder
17. "I'll Be Around"/The Spinners
18. "Inner Smile"/Texas
19. "Into the Groove"/Madonna
20. "Sexbomb"/Tom Jones
21. "Love Train"/The O'Jays
22. "Lovely Day"/Bill Withers
23. "When I Think of You"/Janet Jackson
24. "You Make Me Smile"/Jennifer Love Hewitt
25. "Let's Stay Together"/Al Green
26. "Turn It Up"/Simply Red
27. "No Ordinary Love"/Sade
28. "When Can I See You"/Babyface
29. "U Smile"/Justin Bieber
30. "This Guy's In Love With You"/Steve Tyrell
31. "The Look of Love"/Isaac Hayes
32. "Marry You"/Bruno Mars
33. "Never Gonna Give You Up"/Rick Astley
34. "Dance to the Music"/Sly and the Family Stone
35. "My Life Would Suck Without You"/Kelly Clarkson
36. "The Game of Love"/Santana and Michelle Branch
37. "A Groovy Kind of Love"/Phil Collins
38. "Goin' Out of My Head"/Queen Latifah

39. "Higher Love"/Steve Winwood
40. "I Belong to You"/Lenny Kravitz
41. "I Just Want to Celebrate"/Rare Earth
42. "Can't Get You Out of My Head"/Kylie Minogue
43. "Who's That Lady"/The Isley Brothers
44. "Finally"/CeCe Peniston

The Biologist

I MET THE Biologist in the waiting room of my orthodontist's office when I was in my mid-twenties.

After my teenage years of unexpressed anger, I developed temporomandibular joint disorder, more commonly called TMJ. One summer while visiting my mother, she complained about a clicking that came from my side of the table every time I chewed. Big on table manners, she made it known that this sound was not welcome during her meal.

After several consultations, I formed a plan of action: to wear braces for two years with jaw surgery performed somewhere in between. Come to find out, my upper jaw grew too much and my lower jaw didn't grow far enough, so my mouth never fit properly. The fact that I'd never worn braces as a teenager didn't help either.

Being the only two grown-ups in the waiting room, which was decorated for teenagers with ads of high school football players and cheerleaders, the Biologist and I made eyes at each other, and the next thing I knew we were dating.

He worked in an interactive children's museum, allowing him to dress in Dockers with Birkenstocks. I loved his thick head of messy blond curls, but his teeth were in dire need of straightening. The bottom row looked like a box of spilled Legos dumped on the floor. Coming from a large New England

Catholic family, money was tight when it came to extravagances such as orthodontics.

The Biologist was a real granola guy. By that I mean he ate it for breakfast and preferred a healthy regimen. It was the 1980s, when I dined on a Pepsi and Payday for breakfast most mornings. But once the braces came on, the Payday candy bars had to go. Peanuts and caramel cause major damage to metal mouths.

Being a true tree hugger, he recycled and wasn't much of a consumer. He owned a minimal wardrobe of collared shirts with the museum logo and shorts. And he always moved at a slow and steady pace, never rushed. Tortoise to my hare.

My job kept me hustling. I worked in the promotions department for a new independent television station, which meant there was always something that needed to be promoted. My responsibilities covered writing, producing, and editing thirteen promotional pieces every week. I worked every day. All the time. Sometimes on Saturdays or Sundays. When I worked a short day on the weekends, I'd stop by the museum to pick up the Biologist for dinner. He could be found testing water levels, balancing all twelve aquariums. A makeshift beach housed starfish and sand dollars just below the water, where hermit crabs stumbled about looking for fleas to feast on.

A supersized tank stood in the rear of the exhibit hall with a metal staircase that led to the top of the tank. Unlatching the braided rope, where a sign hung that read Staff Only, I'd climb to the top stairs where the tank had a large opening. I'd roll up my sleeves, kneel down, and put my arms in the tank—all the way up to my elbows—and wait.

It wouldn't take long before Rosy the octopus would find her way over. First a few tentacles would nudge my forearms, wiggling all eight of her arms before grazing the tips of my fingers. She'd tickle my knuckles and palm and wrist. She'd move closer while a whole tentacle caressed my forearm, drawing her nearer toward the heat emitting from my body. When she'd feel safe, one of her suckers would attach to my ulna as if to give me a kiss. Not rough like a hickey. She never left a mark. She swam with the elegance of a dancer. I liked to think Rosy performed the lead in a water ballet, whirling and twirling all eight tentacles about. Sometimes I pretended to be her partner, dancing with her, performing on stage with her.

I think the thing I liked best about the Biologist was my time with Rosy.

Every year I scheduled a trip to visit my mother. At the time she moved a good bit, always living somewhere far away due to my stepfather's occupation, and at that time it was Singapore. This location intrigued the Biologist, and he wanted to come with me. He couldn't wait to investigate Singapore's tropical plants and animals. He also had hopes of having a great time with my mother.

Upon arrival, between unloading the car and unpacking our bags, my mother decided the Biologist wasn't charming and had no manners, and she made it known. She made plans for lunch and dinner that didn't include him, and by day three she flat out told him she didn't think he would make me happy. *Ever*.

She was probably right, but that wasn't her choice to make.

The Biologist booked an earlier flight home, ending our relationship. As much as I loved spending time with Rosy, she wasn't enough to keep us together. I did learn never to allow my mother to meet another man I was interested in until sometime after the engagement.

The Actor

I MET THE Actor while dating the Musician. They were childhood friends.

To say I found the Actor attractive would be an understatement. Whenever I was around the towering, well-coiffed, baby-blue-eyed actor, my heart pounded—no, leapt from my chest. I tingled all over. Everywhere he went, people mistook him for John Travolta. Not only did he know all the dance moves from *Saturday Night Fever*, but he also walked with swagger and a bounce in his step like Tony Manero. But I was crazy in love with the Musician when I met him.

On occasion, the Musician and I would drive home to Charleston from college. While there, we would hang out with the Actor, who still lived there. One day, the Actor asked me to set him up with one of my girlfriends.

So I introduced him to Tiffany, a sorority sister and brief roommate. Six months later, they married and moved to LA so the Actor could work in the film business.

Their marriage lasted three years.

At the time of the Actor's divorce from Tiffany, I learned of the Musician's pending nuptials, and that broke my heart all over again. Somehow, I always thought he would come to his senses and pick me. Magical thinking again. It had been two years since I'd dated the Biologist, and I'd never really gotten over the Musician.

I'd recently quit my career due to burnout from writing and editing promotions all day every day. Exhaustion had become my eau de parfum.

My first job in television was working news—the six and eleven o'clock news for an ABC affiliate in Charleston. My job included studio camera and teleprompter. I hated it and was moved to commercials not long after I started. Working in the commercial department was a nine-to-five job, which became boring fast. I kept my eye on the editors, but there were only two in the entire station. Eventually, I was told that job wouldn't happen for me. So when a new independent station signed on across town, I got the job even though I had never edited.

Since the second TV station was a start-up and product needed to be on the air, my office was a rental. A beat-up old trailer dumped in the parking lot of the station. The entry door rusty and dented from construction sites. The carpeting coffee stained and threadbare. Stale cigarette smoke oozed from the walls. I was told it was only temporary while the interior of the building was under construction. My three to eleven o'clock shift involved watching and editing three movies a night, leaving any nudity and swear words on the floor while placing commercial breaks. In eighteen months, I edited fifteen hundred movies. It became my film school.

When the program director who signed on the Charleston station got a job in Charlotte, he purchased the same movie packages and he took me with him. Here I was promoted to a promo writer/producer/editor. My responsibilities: writing, editing, and mixing thirteen promos every week. Working for a station that was on the air twenty-four hours a day meant twenty-four hours of product needed to be promoted. Six to seven days a week every week became my norm for another three years. I hit a wall and couldn't do any of it anymore.

Instead of checking into a health spa for rest and relaxation, I checked into my grandfather's house in Chapel Hill and took a job waitressing at the Flying Burrito.

The only previous experience I'd had in the restaurant business was during high school, working the drive-through at the local McDonald's. After I had some success in that position, they promoted me to "Star Girl," aka hostess for McDonald's birthday parties. My duties included playing games like Pin the Nose on Ronald McDonald, leading the Ronald McDonald March around the dining area, and serving Happy Meals and birthday cake to guests. Once, I hosted a party for a bunch of adults before they attended an Aerosmith concert. They arrived stoned and turned the Ronald McDonald March into a round of musical chairs.

The Flying Burrito, a local Mexican restaurant, was walking distance from my grandfather's house, and what started as a hostess job immediately turned into the more coveted waitress position. Here I felt like a Star Girl again. Diners sat at my table to have a good time. It was as if I threw a party at each table. I was their personal hostess. But in my brief three months there, a pitcher of beer slid off my tray and onto a lawyer's pin-striped suit because the plastic pitcher was really heavy when it was filled to the top. I ruined every article of clothing I owned, spilling salsa each time someone requested it, which is a lot in a Mexican restaurant. Once, I dumped a steaming hot ultimate burrito smothered in rice and beans on a bald man's head. In my defense, I announced, "Ultimate burrito, ultimate burrito, ultimate burrito!," at the table while the party ignored my need to serve them until the scalding hot plate burned my fingers and I let go and his head was in the way. Some might say I took the restaurant's name literally as burritos and other sundries flew from my fingertips.

So, waitressing wasn't my thing. I knew I needed to get back to editing. Alone in a dark room was where I flourished. And it was the only thing I knew how to do where I wasn't hurting anyone. Not to mention, it paid well. Really well.

♡

Knowing I was out of sorts about the Musician's upcoming marriage, the now-divorced Actor called to console me. It had been two years since his divorce from Tiffany. Tiffany and I never spoke again, but the Actor had called me a couple of times in those two years, catching up on our exes. But something changed after I left my job, and the next thing I knew, he flew east to spend a week with me. We drove to Charleston, where we'd met the first time, ten years earlier.

We played on the swings at Fort Moultrie.

Frolicked through Battery Park and made out as the sun set over the Cooper River Bridge.

I met his parents.

Then we decided . . . I would move to LA.

Sure, I'd never lived with a man before, but I was game. Plus, the Actor and I had known each other for a long time. A whole decade. We liked the same people. And he was hot. *Urban Cowboy* hot! And if I was going to get back into the editing game, Hollywood was my chance to play with the big boys.

In my 1984 Honda Civic Wagon, crammed full with my belongings, and a whopping twelve hundred dollars in my bank account, we began our cross-country trip the day after Christmas. Our first stop was New Orleans, where we noshed on beignets at Cafe du Monde, barhopped on Bourbon Street, and strolled the French Quarter searching for the perfect art to hang in our new home, leaving with a large watercolor of a saxophonist in vibrant colors.

Baton Rouge was only a two-hour drive from New Orleans, and we'd been told Mulate's, the famous Cajun restaurant, was "a not-to-be-missed experience." A barnlike space with large tables seating multiple generations of families of ten or more who dined and danced the fais-dodo together every Saturday night. We feasted on gumbo, crawfish étouffée, and pecan pie before we two-stepped to a squeeze-box, fiddle, and stand-up bass played alongside an old man strumming his worn-out washboard crooning about an alligator named Bubba who lived in the swamp.

From there we drove fourteen hours nonstop across Texas, taking turns sleeping until we pulled into El Paso on New Year's Eve 1990. Frazzled from spending too much time in an enclosed car together, I'd hoped for some alone time in an enormous bathtub. Since we didn't plan ahead, the only available room we could find was at the Splash Motel for $19.95 a night. Our room consisted of a queen bed with a coin machine attached to the headboard that read "Magic Fingers. Four quarters for an hour." I discovered it was broken only after I deposited the four quarters from my change purse. The TV came with rabbit ears, making the reception snowy. And there was no tub for me to decompress. Just a dingy shower with a gray substance on the plastic shower curtain and the tile had green grout. Oh yeah, and I failed to mention that it was located next to a car graveyard, making it feel like the perfect set for a zombie movie.

With no place to escape and nothing left to talk about, the Actor began complaining about the way I packed, my grooming habits, and what I slept in. He asked me if I'd looked for a job yet. Of course I hadn't looked for a job yet. I'd decided to move to California with him on a whim.

He followed that up with he was getting kicked out of the apartment he was living in because he hadn't paid the rent.

Firecracker celebrations boomed outside our dingy motel room while I lay in bed thinking:

Who is this man?
What the hell was I thinking?
Moving in with him?

The Actor was indeed acting. Acting like he had his act together!

I hadn't even gotten to LA and the relationship was over.

Still, I moved in with him to a new place for three months before I called the only person I knew in LA, a director I'd worked with in Charleston, who said, "Come and stay with me."

I packed up all my belongings and slept on the floor of my friend's apartment. Only to have my car stolen, with everything I owned in it, the night before I started my first job in LA.

The Magician

I MET THE Magician at the Magic Castle.

Also known as The Academy of Magical Arts, it's an exclusive club for magicians and their invited guests. You must know a member to get in. So someone who knew someone who knew someone got my name on the list. There is a dress code, which in LA is unheard of since it's a place known for inappropriate attire. Evening dresses and coats with ties only. My friend Frankie had always wanted to go, so she was my plus-one.

The castle itself is an old Victorian mansion in the Hollywood Hills. A magic word must be spoken to enter. I wanna say it was abracadabra, but I'm probably making that up. Once inside, you can't help noticing the dark wood interior throughout the house. All dressed up in our fancy dresses of sparkles and sequins, Frankie and I began our adventure in the main bar. Large curved mirrors and lights decorated the wall behind the bar, reminding me of an old Swensen's ice cream parlor only instead of ice cream, liquor bottles in all shapes and colors lined the counter behind the bar. Ceiling fans swirled from above with wooden owls perched throughout the room onlooking. A tall, slender man with a long nose and spiked bleach blond punk hair appeared beside me out of nowhere dressed in a black dinner jacket and tie. He ordered a round of drinks for Frankie and me and performed a few tricks—one with a deck of cards he pulled out of thin air, the other involving quarters and a dollar bill.

After we oohed and aahed, he put one arm through mine and the other through Frankie's and said, "Follow me." He turned to me and smiled, revealing overcrowded tiny white teeth, and said, "Let me give you a tour."

Our first stop, the Close-Up Room. A mini two-row theater where we watched another magician perform sleight of hand. It was all so impressive. I tried to see how he palmed the cards throughout his performance, but I couldn't because he was so good.

Next, the Magician escorted us to the Houdini Chamber, where private séances are held. A huge round table filled the room. Red velvet curtains draped the window. Oil paintings and Harry Houdini memorabilia decorated the blood-red walls. I closed my eyes tight and tried to conjure up Houdini's spirit, but the only thing that showed up was a waitress wondering if I wanted another drink.

After the big show in the main theater, where an illusionist performed with boxes and mirrors, the Magician decided to impress me one last time, leading us downstairs to the "members-only" library where one-of-a-kind books on magic filled over-stacked shelves. He described the collection while we stood just outside the velvet rope. I rubbernecked the best I could but couldn't make out any of the titles. Frankie tagged along, understanding now that he was interested in me, and made kissy-face sounds when she thought the Magician wasn't looking.

It was a magical evening, and before it ended, the Magician asked to see me again. *This could be fun*, I thought as I gave him my number. He kissed me on the cheek, and we said good night.

♡

Since the Magician performed nights, our dates happened during the day. Turned out he loved spending time with celebrities. Dead celebrities. So our first date was at the Forest Lawn Glendale cemetery, where we called on Walt Disney, Lon Chaney, and Humphrey Bogart. We had a great time walking through the palatial park discussing our favorite films. Our next date took place at the infamous Hollywood Forever Cemetery. It's a beautiful graveyard right across from Paramount. If I were going to be buried, that's the location I would choose, but I'm not. I'm going to be cremated. Here, we paid our final respects to Judy Garland and Douglas Fairbanks, who, according to the brochure, had "a reflection pool" in front of his mammoth monument of a tombstone. It looked more like a lap pool to me. It took us a while to find Rudolph Valentino, who lay tucked away in a vault—just a metal placard among many on a wall filled with dozens. Then, right after, we stopped by next door and said hello to Lucille Ball and Liberace at Forest Lawn Hollywood.

Then one day, not long after another outing to the Pierce Brothers Westwood cemetery, where we hung out with Marilyn Monroe and Truman Capote, the Magician disappeared.

Never to be seen again.

Best magic trick ever.

"I almost had a psychic girlfriend, but she left me before we met."

—Steven Wright

Rollerblading Dad

FOUR MONTHS AFTER MY last sighting of the Magician, I sat next to Rollerblading Dad in business class on a flight from New York to Los Angeles.

Tall, balding, and English, he was polite and could carry on a conversation for five hours all the way to the West Coast. Among the many things I learned about him was he rollerbladed every day on the beach. And he had a nine-year-old son named Charlie. Before we parted, he asked for my number. I thought, *My mom lives in London, so we have that in common. Why not?*

I was in my thirties by then and had recently been secretly smitten with another Englishman, Spencer, who worked as an art director at an advertising agency, but he didn't even know I existed. Whenever I had the opportunity to start a conversation with Spencer, my knees buckled, and when I opened my mouth, nothing came out. I felt nauseous and wanted to throw up. That's what I thought love felt like—getting off the Scrambler ride at the amusement park, dizzy and nauseous. Years later I would take those same signs as ones that should make me run as far from the person as I could get.

Anyway, turned out, Rollerblading Dad lived on the Westside of LA where I lived, which is unusual when you meet someone on a plane heading to LAX. They're usually flying off to somewhere else. And not only did Rollerblading Dad live on the Westside, but he also lived on the same street as Spencer.

Actually, he lived next door! LA can be such a small world sometimes.

Rollerblading Dad worked in the auto parts business and was not work focused at all. Something I had not experienced with any of the men I'd dated in Los Angeles. They were all working their way up in the entertainment business, which meant they were working or networking every moment of every day like I was.

♡

A few months into our relationship, Rollerblading Dad decided it would be a good idea to take me bike riding through the Marina. I wasn't keen on it with athleticism not being my thing, but I figured I'd give it a whirl, only to wipe out on a bunch of gravel the first twenty minutes in, ripping the skin off of my right calf. There was no way I could ride my bike back to his house. So I waited while it took him over an hour to return with a car.

"I think I need to see a doctor," I said as I hopped on one foot to the passenger seat, blood oozing from my skin, dripping toward my ankle, staining my new super-white socks.

He gave my huge gash a quick glance before he threw the bike in the back of his SUV and said, "You'll be fine."

I washed it off the best I could, but a few days later my boss looked at it and said, "The color is off. It doesn't look good. You need to have that checked out."

I did. It was infected.

♡

Rollerblading Dad had full custody of his nine-year-old son, which meant parenting for him went from three in the afternoon until eight the next morning. As soon as Charlie was on his way to school, it was time for him to hit the beach and rollerblade. For two hours every day.

On occasion, Rollerblading Dad cooked dinner, pasta out of a jar or mac and cheese from a box, which we ate at their dinner table while Charlie shared his successes or the PE activity of the day. At nine, Charlie oozed sweetness and gave me good-night hugs.

This was the first time I'd ever dated a man with a child. All the men I'd dated before had still been children themselves.

Four months into our relationship, and after a few margaritas downed at the Cheesecake Factory in Marina del Rey, Rollerblading Dad got down on one knee in the parking lot and proposed in front of a bunch of strangers who all stopped to watch.

"Marry me!" he shouted from a bended knee, in shorts on a hot pavement, while he reached for my right hand.

"Get up," I whispered, my jaw clenched while trying to yank this lanky man to his feet.

"I'll make you happy," he slurred as he wobbled on his bended knee.

Just beyond him, a family of five from Milwaukee wearing "Go Bucks" hats and T-shirts stopped and stared like they were catching a matinee performance. The wife's mouth gaped open. Two young women stumbled out of the restaurant and giggled with excitement when they saw us.

"I'm not doing this here," I announced, grinding my teeth. "Get up!"

Shame and embarrassment smothered me as heat emitted from the black tar parking lot, flushing my face and drenching me in perspiration. He had become sloppy from drinking, which made him so unattractive. Desperation reeked from his sweat.

Eventually, he relented and allowed me to drag him to his feet and carried on like a good English boy with a smile on his face all the way back to the car.

"I think it would be lovely if we got married," he said as he tried to jam his seat belt fastener in several times but kept missing the click due to his one too many drinks. "Don't you?"

"I don't." I turned the key in the ignition, starting up the car, and looked at him. His posture shifted—shoulders folding in, head down as this information began to sober him up.

As I sat and watched him, I realized I had chosen the Actor again. Fun and fly by the seat of his pants. But with the proposal, reality sank in. He was not nurturing to me, not in the way I wanted or needed. And Rollerblading Dad needed someone to support him financially and emotionally, and I was in no way ready to do either.

I found out later Charlie was heartbroken over my breakup with his father. Something I'd never even considered, that his child liked me enough to be sad I'd left. Maybe I hadn't thought of the possibility because I never liked anyone my father dated and would have been greatly relieved if one day they had just disappeared, never to be seen again.

But Charlie taught me that other hearts—tiny, fragile hearts—get involved in relationship dynamics too. And that someone else could and did love me.

Tea Time

SOMETIME AROUND THREE in the afternoon, with the temperature well over 100 degrees, I found myself in the garage looking deep into a very large box containing 1,000 battery-operated tea lights. I purchased this many to light the outskirts of the vineyard. I was about 250 tea lights in, another 750 to go, with the ceremony clocking in at T-minus two hours and thirty minutes.

I had designed a method of turning each one on and then dumping it in a plastic bag. When I'd fill up the bag, I'd run around the vineyard, placing them in walkways, staircases, and thoroughfares to illuminate after the sun had set. My right thumb, now raw from having flipped the switch underneath the tea lights, was moving slower, and I had moved to trying to turn them on left-handed, which slowed the process even more.

Dad arrived with Thelma and Louise dressed in their wedding attire and joined in. My own sweatshop in the garage.

I should have hired a wedding coordinator.

The Ghoster

I MET THE Ghoster on a blind date.

Sometime in my mid-thirties, while living in Brentwood, my boss's father set me up.

The Ghoster wore a suit during the day while wining and dining me at night. With thick brown hair and blue eyes that sparkled like marbles in the sun, all he had to do was smile at me from across the table and I melted. Into my chair. Like garlic butter on toasted bread. I was done. In love.

On our first date he drove us to a cozy, romantic restaurant by the beach. He opened my car door, pulled out my chair, and stood up when I went to the ladies' room. At the end of the night, he walked me to my front door. A real gentleman. The next day he called and sent flowers. We dined at fancy spots in Beverly Hills and Malibu, where he lived, ending each evening in his hot tub overlooking the Pacific Ocean watching Santa Monica twinkle in the night like the inside of Tiffany's on Rodeo Drive.

A few months in he flew me to Vegas, where, swept up in the moment of grand fountains, endless crab legs, and Wayne Newton, he said, "Marry me! Marry me!" My heart pounded. I wanted to say yes, but I smiled and said, "It's too soon."

We celebrated Christmas with his family in Santa Barbara. I met his mother, his sister, and his brother-in-law. They played tennis. We walked on the beach and caught *Jerry Maguire* at the local theater.

A month later, when I opened my front door, he stood there holding my coffee maker that I'd taken to his house months before.

"I'm going to be out of town, so I thought I'd bring you your coffee maker."

"Okay," I said, setting my coffee maker on the coffee table just inside the door.

We had a lovely dinner.

Then he ghosted me.

The Divorcée

WHEN I BOUGHT my first condo in my thirties, an older divorced friend who lived in a tiny upstairs studio apartment said, "I thought buying a home was something you did when you got married."

The Unavailable Men

I MET THE first Unavailable Man at work.

He was the very first Englishman I fell for, being flirty and quite the charmer. An engineer, hired to help us start up a new independent television station. His job was to get the transmitter up and running.

There were five managers and me. I was the first employee. Coming from an editing background, I was hired in the engineering department, and in order to meet FCC requirements to get our license, we had to be "on air" four hours a day. It was decided we'd air two old movies, commercial free, from seven to eleven every night seven days a week.

In the beginning, my job consisted of driving out to the country where the transmitter sat in the middle of a cow pasture. Upon arrival each evening at five o'clock, I'd begin my job turning on a bunch of switches that allowed the transmitter to warm up. Then just before seven, I'd queue up a movie and hit play, allowing the first film to run without interruption. Just before the first film ended, I'd queue up the second one to run immediately after while taking readings of the transmitter gauges and monitors until the second film ended. By eleven I'd shut down the transmitter and begin my commute home.

Having just moved to a new town and ending my seven-year relationship with the Musician, I was lonely. When the Englishman arrived on the scene, I was happy. I looked forward to having someone handsome to talk to. In the middle of nowhere in a tiny box that sheltered the electronics of the transmitter, this chap with a gregarious personality had a captivated audience.

After having my days free when everyone else was working, he'd brighten each evening. Pretty soon, broadcasting movies wasn't the only thing being emitted from our transmitter.

A few weeks into dating, he let it slip that he had children.

And then while we were still in bed sharing a cup of coffee early one morning, his wife called. Being so inexperienced in the world, my skin slithered with grime and dirt. I wanted to scrub my skin off. Shame hovered around me. Who does that? Cheat on his wife? A man with children!

I cried for a few days, vacillating between shame and disgust.

Eventually, his job ended and he returned to England.

Cheerio!

The next Unavailable Man I also met at work.

He and his wife didn't live together. In fact, they lived in different states. Only saw each other on the weekends. He did all the driving. She never drove to see him, so I saw him during the week and had my weekends all to myself. Being still young and stupid, though, my view had changed since the English Unavailable Man. This time, I wasn't ashamed of dating a married man. I thought he was the one who made the commitment, not me. And working in a dark room alone day in and day out, who else did I meet but married men in the office.

Then for my birthday, he bought me lingerie.

That's when I realized it was all about him.

So I moved on.

The third and last Unavailable Man I spent time with, I also met at work.

He was powerful and made tons of money, but after finally spending a weekend together, I thought, *This isn't fun. It's all about him.*

Not one of those men made me feel like I was special. None of them even helped me in my career. They were totally unavailable, reflecting back to me my own unavailability.

The Wedding Menu

Passed Hors d'Oeuvres:

Grilled Lambsicles with Lemongrass Mint Dipping Sauce

Mini Pulled Pork Sandwiches on Sweet Hawaiian Rolls

Seared Rare Tri-Tip Crostini with Arugula and Horseradish Aioli

Mini Mushroom Tartlets

Mini Goat Cheese and Oven Roasted Tomato Tarts

Caprese Skewers

Herb Roasted Fingerling Potatoes with Garlic Aioli

Grazing Table:

Cheese and Charcuterie Platter (Brie, Chunks of Cheeses, Soppressata, Salami, Chorizo), Grapes, Dried Apricots, Walnuts, Olives, Figs, Fig Jam (on marble)

Spiced Nuts (in wood cups)

Crudités Basket on Wheatgrass with Dill Dip

Mixed Berries and Cream (in shot glasses with spoons)

Coffee/Cream/Sugar

Strawberry Lemonade (in dispenser)

Cucumber with Mint Water (in dispenser)

Fancy Dog Biscuits for Ron Howard

My Longest Relationship

I MET HIM in Santa Monica on Montana and Fifteenth.

Forty-one and still single, I asked Santa for the perfect guy. Someone handsome, loving, and kind. I knew someone my age should be asking God or my Higher Power for something as big as that, but it happened to be around the holidays, so I thought, why not ask Santa?

When he didn't deliver, I went to the internet.

After surfing, discarding, and editing, I kept going back to one profile. He had thick strawberry blond hair and big brown eyes. Late at night, I lost myself staring at his profile pic.

Finally, I sent an email asking if we could meet. We set a date for the weekend.

Saturday morning after breakfast, I arrived on time.

He was standing next to an older lady who was holding a Chihuahua wearing a red polka-dot dress—the dog, not the older lady.

My heart pounded as I introduced myself. He was charismatic as he grazed my arm.

He wanted to take a walk around the block, north of Montana with all its big fancy houses and lawns. I lusted after the homes while he noticed each tree we passed, taking his time to stop at each one. I noticed when people walked by, they would look at him—he was a real head turner.

The breeze in the air rustled what leaves remained in the bushes and trees while rays of sunshine spilled down on us, making the day joyful. There was a comfortableness in our silence.

Over the next few weeks, he did everything I wanted to do. Went everywhere I wanted to go. A match made in heaven. Eventually, I leaned into doing things he wanted to do, like going for longer walks and playing ball, even when I didn't feel like it. But that's what love does. It makes you want to do things you wouldn't have wanted to do.

He was the best listener. It didn't matter if I wanted to rant about someone behaving badly at the office or drone on and on about someone who didn't behave the way I thought they should. He listened until I had had enough of myself. He was patient that way.

He wasn't big on PDA, thank God. I dislike all that kissing and public displays of affection. He didn't snore or hog the covers. And he was the best cuddler! I've heard it said that all a girl really wants is a snuggle and to be heard. And for others to adore the one she's with. There was a lightness to his swagger that spoke confidence. His whiskers were dark against his thick strawberry blond mane. I never tired of running my fingers through it. He was the only one I wanted to hang out with.

My dog, Ron Howard.

IT Guy

I MET IT Guy on Match.com.

Lofty with a dyed bowl haircut and freckles everywhere, IT Guy seemed smitten from the moment we met over a cup of coffee. By now, I had Ron Howard in my life, and he went everywhere with me, including on my dates. They were polite on their first meeting, giving each other plenty of space.

IT Guy worked as an independent contractor in the computer programming world doing things I never understood, but in LA, where everyone carries different area codes, dating someone in the same zip code was an anomaly. Normally when I dated someone who lived ten miles away, I would drive an hour each way. So when I found out he lived two blocks from me, it was like winning the lottery!

I was in my forties, and Ron Howard and I walked to work, walking past IT Guy's home twice a day on our way to and from the office.

Sometimes we'd stop by on our way home. IT Guy liked to cook, so he'd make dinner. We'd sit at a two-top bar-height round table bumped up against his tiny kitchen wall. Ron Howard liked to lie in his spot on the linoleum kitchen floor beside my chair while we dined. After dinner, Ron would rest on the floor next to the sofa while we watched television. He'd wait patiently on the other side of the bedroom door when we had sex only to reside the rest of the evening on the floor next to my side of the bed until dawn.

After a couple of months, I knew a lot about IT Guy. He used Just for Men H-25 light brown hair color shampoo and British Sterling aftershave. He liked to watch James Bond movies on his well-worn chestnut-colored velour sofa.

I thought I knew him well enough to invite Ron Howard up on the sofa.

In my peripheral vision, IT Guy glared over at me while saying, "I don't think your dog belongs on the couch."

"What?" I shook my head as if I'd misheard him.

"I don't think dogs belong on the couch."

"You don't . . ."

"I don't think dogs belong on furniture."

"You're kidding, right?"

"Actually, I don't even think dogs belong in the house."

I blinked, my brain spinning like a spirograph trying to make sense of what I had just heard. From a man I'd gotten naked with. I began to itch as if I had just contracted lice. "You don't think my dog belongs in your house?"

"I don't think dogs belong in the house."

I reached for Ron's leash on the coffee table, attached it to his harness, and slammed the front door on the way out.

A few days later, I got an email from IT Guy telling me he missed me.

I didn't respond. I preferred sleeping with Ron. He didn't snore, took up less of the bed, and had better table manners.

My Biggest Worry

MY BIGGEST WORRY as a single gal: I would die alone in my townhouse and no one would know, leaving Ron Howard unfed and unwalked for days.

The Ghoster Returns

RIGHT AROUND MY fortieth birthday, while I lived in Santa Monica, I came home to a message on my answering machine. I recognized the voice right away as the guy who'd told me he loved me. Wanted to marry me. And then left without a word.

"My son found a photo of us taken in Vegas and asked who you were. I told him you were the one who got away."

My heart galloped, like a racehorse out the gate, as I listened to the message, remembering his blue eyes that sparkled blinding light when he smiled at me.

"Please call me."

I held my breath, trying to hold in the flood of feelings that began to drown me. Pulling me under, in feelings of loneliness and abandonment from the way things ended. All the way down to disappointment in how he had ended it. Ditching me without a word. Who does that?

I wanted to dial those digits. Excited to be wanted again. To have been thought about through the years. To be the one he always wanted.

But he hurt me. Vanished without an explanation. Taking years to get over him. To move on.

But I wanted an explanation, so I picked up the phone and called him back.

We had dinner.

He'd moved to Thousand Oaks, where he had become a divorced dad.

I met his son.
He met Ron Howard.
He told me I was the one.
A month later, he disappeared again . . .

"All discarded lovers should be given a second chance, but with somebody else."

—Mae West

The Gym Rat

I MET THE Gym Rat at a party.

Over-tanned, all muscle, and inked everywhere, most notably a rat on his left bicep. Two front teeth hung from its mouth while its tail wrapped around his forearm. It was very realistic. No resemblance to Mickey at all. He owned a small elite gym in Beverly Hills that was open for clients only when he himself wasn't working out, which wound up being a couple of hours in the late mornings after his own six-mile run. Then a few hours before his second personal workout, two hours on a stationary bike, before he'd train a couple of people right after regular work hours.

The Gym Rat was a creature of habit, eating canned salmon and a head of cabbage every night for dinner. He was this way about sex too. The same every single time we did it—always in my bed, missionary style. And being all muscle, he weighed a ton. It wasn't fun.

He drove a bright yellow Corvette and rode a matching Harley even though he couldn't afford the rent on his studio apartment in West LA. Oh, and he hadn't left town in thirty years. Thirty years!

A life no bigger than five miles? Salmon and cabbage every night?

I wanted stability, but I'd prefer to be on my own over boredom any day.

Married to My Job

SOMETIME IN MY forties, I was having lunch with one of my clients. We'd worked several jobs together over the years, so I felt like we knew each other.

"What are you doing this weekend?" I asked.

"The wife and I are going to celebrate our wedding anniversary."

"Congratulations! Where are you going?"

"Santa Barbara."

"How fabulous! I hope to do that one day."

"Do what?" he asked, cocking his head to one side with a quizzical look.

"Celebrate a wedding anniversary."

"Really? I always thought of you as a career girl."

"I just never met the right guy," I said, "so I wound up spending all my time at work."

Sibling Math

I HAVE A sister.

She's eight years younger.

She married ten years before I did—to a man twenty-two years her senior.

She dated him for four years.

Then she had a secret wedding at her soon-to-be eighty-eight-year-old mother-in-law's house two days after Christmas. Secret in that she didn't invite our parents.

Twenty years later . . . they're still happily married.

I have a half brother.

We share the same father.

He's fifteen years younger than me.

He married twelve years before I did.

To a woman eight years older than he is.

They had two beautiful girls and one really handsome boy.

They are still a happily married couple.

I have a stepbrother.

He's six years younger than me.

He met his wife online in 2003.

My stepbrother became a stepfather to a son.

My stepbrother and his wife are still happily married.

I think my siblings add up to a lot of hope.

The Introduction

HE ARRIVED VIA email in my inbox through the Plenty of Fish dating website.

It was a form letter. Really? *So generic, no imagination*, I thought, and I tossed it in the trash.

The next day an exact copy of the original email arrived in my inbox again. Seriously. Did he forget he already sent me one? He was like a Realtor canvassing a neighborhood. If this guy couldn't take the time to write me a personal note, I couldn't be bothered to respond. Into the trash.

On the third day, he apparently got the hint. Another email arrived. It read:

Dear Santa Monica Catch,
You reeled me in with your smile, and I stayed because your profile page made me laugh. Plus, I noticed you haven't responded to my previous two form emails, so I thought I'd try one last time with a personal approach. I think we should meet. Have a bite to eat.

He signed off, "The Reel McCoy aka Chris Johnson aka 'Big Johnson.'"

I never eat on the first date. I don't even do coffee. Too much of a commitment. I tried it once when I didn't know any better, and the guy who showed up was unrecognizable. He didn't look like his photo at all, so much so that when we met I thought I was meeting his father. He was completely gray with age spots. So I started to suggest a first date be a walk with Ron Howard. That way I could see if they were who they said they were, and no money or time had to be exchanged while Ron Howard got to take care of business.

I studied his profile again. The Reel McCoy.

As a federal prosecutor, he took down Asian and Russian gangs.

I'd just returned from editing a movie in China.

He'd been a JAG.

My father was in the navy. My brother in the air force.

And The Reel McCoy was from the South, so we had that in common too.

He said he weighed more than he should. He looked overweight in his profile picture.

He lived in the Valley, where it all looks the same. Strip malls everywhere, 7-Elevens on every corner, and 20 degrees hotter than the beach on any given day.

I wasn't sure.

He said his name was Johnson. How scary could he be with such an ordinary name?

It's just a meal. We can talk about China and the navy. And I do like to eat. I'll just have an appetizer.

The Walk

T-MINUS FIFTEEN MINUTES.

Peering out the upstairs window, I spied on the guests below. Women in flowered dresses chatted while wiping perspiration from their brows and underarms. My oldest friend, Snapper, arrived donning a green pin-striped seersucker suit. His parents bestowed that nickname when he was three because he spent his preschool years biting other children. And it stuck, following him right into middle age. I'd only known him as Snapper for years until one day he showed me his driver's license. His legal name: Cleatis. My old workmate Julie had picked up a palm leaf somewhere and waved it at her boyfriend like she was back in Egyptian times and he was some sort of pharaoh. Everyone else held a glass of the spa water while they scouted out the best place to stand in the shade, which, on a vineyard, there isn't any. Frankie placed the last of the thousand tea lights along the railway ties around the patio.

I pulled my hair into a high ponytail and showered, then sat at my makeup table and applied sunscreen, blush, and mascara while Ron Howard lay on the tail of my cathedral-length veil.

"It's a new adventure for you and me."

His ears turned toward me. And he tilted his head. I could always count on Ron listening, and I'm pretty sure he understood every word I uttered.

Stepping into my long gown, I struggled to get it on. Unable to zip the back of my dress, I opened the bedroom door, where Dad stood waiting for me.

He pulled the zipper together tight with his arthritic hands. I inhaled the best I could, sucking in the excess I'd put on since my last fitting.

"There. Can you breathe?" Dad asked, hooking the last hook.

"Who needs to breathe? I'm finally getting married."

We both busted out laughing.

"I'm happy for you." He put his hand on my upper arm and looked me in the eyes. His baby blues, though tired, sparkled with delight. "Really happy for you." He wrapped his arms around me and hugged me before reminding us, "It's time to go. The wedding started five minutes ago." Always punctual, my father expected the same from me. "If you're not early, you're late." One was never late in the navy.

I slipped into my glittered shoes, grabbed my veil, and placed the comb just above my ponytail. Ron Howard jumped into my arms so I could carry him down the staircase, allowing the photographer a few snaps along the way, with Dad close behind toting my cascading white lily bouquet.

Standing inside behind the door that led to the patio where all the guests were melting, Frankie cued the DJ. The first few notes of "At Last" played as I put Ron Howard down beside me. He looked so cute in his tuxedo tie. I turned and smiled at my father. He stood proud, his shoulders back as if he were at attention. Then he grinned back at me before handing me my bouquet.

"You ready?"

"Let's go."

The door opened. Heat barreled toward me, smacking me in the face as I stepped onto the patio. The hot air so thick and heavy it felt like walking into a sauna. A stranger in a sequined dress no bigger than a cloth napkin greeted us with a smile. She was someone's guest and now obviously mine. I gave her my stink eye before trying to find a friendly face.

Click click click. A mob of friends surrounded us like paparazzi. Their phones and cameras in our faces. As we moved forward, my friends walked backward holding their cameras, swirling around like bees to a hive. Each trying to get the perfect picture.

"What's going on?" Dad screamed over Etta singing, "My lonely days are over." I could tell by the tone of his voice he wasn't happy

"Daddy, they're so excited to finally see me get married." I smiled.

"Geeze," he swore as he maneuvered me toward Big Johnson.

Dad delivered me to the front, kissed my cheek, and took a seat in the front row between Thelma and Louise. Ron and I stood with Big Johnson's daughters on each side of us, and the judge began. Not only did my dress impinge on my breathing, but so did my fear. Big Johnson sensed my nervousness, reached down, and took my hand, holding it with such tenderness and love. He was going all in. With me. He held no fear. His love for me was real. And I knew this man wanted to spend the rest of his life with me.

The Meeting

I MET BIG Johnson at a seafood restaurant walking distance from my home.

Wearing a brown-and-yellow-checkered shirt with jeans, he looked like his photographs: big and tall, like a defensive lineman who hadn't stepped foot in a gym in over ten years. He greeted me by holding open the front door. It was refreshing to stand next to someone so tall in Los Angeles. Everyone in this city is wafer-thin and Lilliputian-esque.

At eleven thirty on a Sunday morning, the eatery was empty, giving our meeting an air of intimacy. Big Johnson stood next to the table and waited until I slid into my side of the booth. Then he did his best to slip into the booth across the table from me. His shirt buttons strained across his stomach as they wedged against the table. He smiled while he adjusted himself. I feigned interest in the bartender wiping the rims of the wineglasses and then stacking them in a huge cabinet where the liquor bottles twinkled from the morning light.

As the waitress handed us our menus, Big Johnson announced, "I come here for the lobster bisque."

I smiled.

"It's some of the best I've ever had."

I glanced at the menu and decided on a shrimp cocktail before I took a good look at him. Aquamarine eyes sparkled back at me through his dated generic gold-wire frames. Thick, wavy brown hair chopped short framed his round face.

"So, what do you think of online dating?" he asked, putting down his menu.

"I tried other sites in the past, but you're my first this go-round. I've never had any success. But this time, I'd really like to meet someone. Someone to spend the rest of my life with."

"I've tried spending the rest of my life with someone a couple of times and it didn't last. I'm hoping the third time is a charm." He smiled. "You're prettier than your photographs."

"Thank you." I smiled.

"And you have the most beautiful smile." His Diet Pepsi arrived, and he took a sip.

"Thank you." *He's really charming, but the Valley, I don't know.* "How long did it take you to get to Santa Monica today?"

"Depends on traffic. Twenty-five minutes today, but it's the weekend. It can take a lot longer in rush hour."

"I hate driving. I find it so stressful." I shook out my paper napkin and placed it in my lap.

"I like driving. I listen to books on tape."

"Do you read?"

He took another swig of his Diet Pepsi before he said, "I listen to two to three books a month. Does that count?"

"I'm not sure." I hadn't listened to many books, but it was becoming all the rage.

"Well, I've been listening to books since 1991 when I moved here and had to commute. So I guess I was ahead of my time."

When the food arrived, Big Johnson crushed up his saltine crackers and stirred them into his lobster bisque while he told me about his time as a JAG in Guantanamo, working as a federal prosecutor in Kowloon and Kiev, and growing up in Pearl Harbor and Champaign, Illinois, among other places the family moved to since his father was a colonel in the marines.

While I nibbled on my shrimp cocktail, I told him about my adventures working in China, editing what the director believed to be the first telling of the Cinderella story in Mandarin with an all-Chinese crew, and what a life-changing experience it had been for me. How I had moved around a lot, too, as a kid, and how much I loved living in LA.

Big Johnson shared that he was in the process of constructing his house in the Valley, planting a vineyard with 225 Silver Oak Cabernet replacement vines that would be ready for their first harvest that fall.

Before I knew it, our waitress was busing our table and it was time to leave.

Outside the restaurant, we lingered on the sidewalk.

"We could continue this tomorrow night over dinner if you'd like," he offered, leaning in for a kiss.

I gently pushed him away.

"I'm not ready for that, but I might be able to make it through another meal with you." I smiled and blinked. "You are very interesting," I flirted.

Big Johnson grinned. "See you tomorrow night. I'll call you with details." Having scored a second date, he strutted off toward his car.

The Callback

THE NEXT NIGHT, we dined at the same restaurant. This time on the back patio under fairy lights that hung above the outdoor furniture. A warm breeze of garlic and grilled fish provided more ambiance. *He must really like the lobster bisque to dine here again*, I thought. Or maybe this was just his lucky date spot.

This time, there was a comfortableness, yet I noticed that I was noticeably uncomfortable with his size. I had never been with a man as big as he was. He took up a lot of space.

After dinner, we strolled down Main Street. He stopped and kissed me in front of the Circle Bar. We took up the whole sidewalk.

He was moving fast, and I wasn't ready for this. I needed to get to know him better before all this PDA.

The Ghoster Returns, Again

TWO DAYS AFTER our second date, the Ghoster found me on Plenty of Fish. I know. Crazy, right? What was he doing on this site? Why did he have to contact me again? Why did I want to see him again? Unfinished business with so many questions—what can I say?

So, I called Big Johnson and told him, "I need to find out what happened. I hope you understand."

"I really like you," he sighed through the phone. "If it doesn't work out, call me."

♡

The Ghoster told me in his email that he'd gotten his life together. That he needed to see me.

The next night, we had dinner at Ivy at the Shore.

A week later, he impressed my mother and stepfather with dinner at Capo, where he told them he wanted to spend the rest of his life with me.

We flew to Phoenix for the day and had lunch with his father.

Made plans to fly out to the East Coast to meet my father.

I took down my profile.

And then, three months later, he was gone again. Without a word.

Same shit, different year.

"Dating an ex is the equivalent of failing a test you already had the answers to."

—Kendrick Cole

The Do-Over

BACK IN THE ocean for me.

A few months after putting my profile back up, an email landed in my inbox. "So, it didn't work out with that old love? How about lunch tomorrow?"

When I arrived at our usual restaurant, Big Johnson arranged for us to sit in our first-date booth and we picked up where we left off.

He never stopped grinning while his eyes sparkled as he talked over a large bowl of lobster bisque, occasionally stirring in more saltines after crushing them in his fist.

"What do you have going on this weekend?" he asked before he blew over his steaming hot soup spoon.

"What are you thinking?" I liked how he was diving right back in and not grilling me about where I'd been and why I hadn't called.

"Well, my girls just left for Barcelona for three weeks with their mom, so I was thinking of driving up to Napa. I need to see how their grapes are doing so I know what to do with mine. Wanna go for a few days?"

I thought about it for a moment.

I had nothing going on for the next few days.

And I enjoyed spending time with him.

"Okay," I said. "And you can teach me about wine."

The Sleepover

IT WAS DECIDED I would spend the night at Big Johnson's place, aka Big Johnson Winery, so we could get a good head start the following morning for our grand adventure to Napa Valley.

Now, I'd never traveled north of Mulholland, east of the 405, or south of LAX, so when it was decided that we would depart from the Valley, I packed a snack and a sweater, along with food and a leash for Ron Howard.

Yes, I had GPS, but LA is a sprawling county, and I wanted to be prepared.

After taking the 10 west to the 405 north to the 101 north, I exited Shoup. Crossing Ventura Boulevard, I veered right onto several winding roads leading up in the hills. With each right, the road changed names. When I finally turned left on a no-name dirt road, my GPS dropped out of network. The dirt road turned out to be a fire road covered in overgrown, thorny weeds. When I climbed out of my car to catch a signal, the weeds reached out to scratch me like a cloud of irate cats. I clung to the edge of the road, where I paced in small circles in front of my VW Beetle until I had service.

"Uh, hi!" I said when Big Johnson picked up.

"You're here! I'll be right down." There was excitement in his voice.

"I'm afraid not, I'm on a dirt road. My GPS went out. I drove till I saw a sign that says 'Fire road no parking.'" I looked around for any markers to give him.

"I think you wound up on Ostrich Drive," he said. "I know where you are. Hang tight. I'll come get you."

Ten minutes later, Big Johnson rescued me, having hiked down the fire road, and then he drove us back to his place.

Finally, I arrived at Big Johnson Winery, surviving the road less traveled.

That night we dined at a fancy steak house in Woodland Hills before returning to his house, where I got a tour of Big Johnson Winery that ended with a grand finale: taking off our clothes and discovering we did have chemistry. Yes, indeed, we did.

The Next Morning

I AWOKE TO the sound of a soda can opening.

"Coffee, I need coffee," I pleaded after an evening of decadence.

"How do you like it?" he asked with a smile.

"With almond milk. Mostly milk—latte-like."

Big Johnson took a sip from his Diet Pepsi and hopped out of bed, throwing on last night's clothes. Once dressed, he leaned over and kissed my cheek. "What would you like with your almond milk latte?"

"Blueberry muffins and cinnamon rolls are my favorite," I informed him as if I were filling out a more intimate profile. I rolled over on my back and adjusted my pillow to better support my neck. Big Johnson picked up Ron Howard and placed him in bed with me.

"You enjoy lounging in bed with Ron Howard, and I'll be right back."

I closed my eyes and thought, *I think I'm gonna like it here.*

The Boy Scout

BIG JOHNSON'S A great driver.
And he's prepared.
Loose change in the console for parking meters.
Snacks and water in the back of the car.
Plus, he stops for a bathroom break anytime I ask.
He even likes my playlist of Steve Winwood, Sade, and Seal.
He's a great travel companion.

The Rounds

WE BEGAN AT Opus One with a glass of Cabernet. Sat on a bench overlooking the vineyard.

Then Silver Oak. Since Big Johnson's vineyard was filled with their Cabernet replacement vines, we spent time asking questions—about watering, pruning, and netting—all while holding hands.

Mustards served a delicious lunch. I ordered baby back ribs with a side of pasta carbonara. Wine tasting can make a girl hungry.

Then we stopped at Frog's Leap,

Stag's Leap,

and Duckhorn, followed by dinner under the stars.

The Next Day

OUR THIRD DAY kicked off with breakfast on the patio under a huge oak tree.

We met my friend who worked at Cakebread.

She gave us a tour of their cellar.

Introduced us to their winemaker.

We drank a flight.

Big Johnson bought a case.

He gave a bottle to my friend.

He's thoughtful, generous, and kind.

The Takedown

AS I SAT passenger side in the late afternoon while we headed south down the 5 toward LA, Big Johnson asked, "Well, what do you think? Should we take our profiles down?"

"We've got two more weeks before your girls return, and I'm having fun." I pulled out my phone and looked at my profile. It was the best one I'd ever written. "You sure you don't want to give it another week or so?"

"I'm good. I don't need to make a date with anyone but you."

I looked at my profile one more time. "Okay. I'm in!"

Big Johnson took the next exit and pulled into the In-N-Out parking lot, and together we deleted "Santa Monica Catch" and "The Reel McCoy," signifying these two fish had been caught.

The Poop

"LOVE IS SOMETHING beyond the excitement of romance and being in love. It is a committed, thoughtful decision," the judge read.

Big Johnson squeezed my hand, turned toward me, and smiled.

I smiled back. He looked handsome in his pin-striped suit.

The judge continued, "It is the wish of everyone here today that your marriage brings you much happiness. Happiness in marriage doesn't just happen, though. You must work on it. Remember to say 'I love you,' to hold hands whenever you get the chance, and at no time to take the other for granted."

I looked at Big Johnson's boutonniere on his lapel. It was a large orchid with a piece of greenery behind it, and just above it on his shoulder, a bird had taken a dump. He had bird poop on his suit. I studied the deposit and smiled while I remembered that in England it's considered good luck.

The Gas Station Attendant

THE MORNING AFTER we'd taken down our profiles, I rolled over in Big Johnson's bed to a perfect latte having been delivered to me by Big Johnson a few minutes earlier.

Then before he went to check on the vines, he said, "Every time you drive out to see me, I'll fill your tank up with gas and wash your car."

Who is this man? Is he for real?

The Hustler

AFTER WE RETURNED from Napa, Big Johnson wanted to show off his neighborhood, show me how "cool" the Valley was, so we began the evening at his local bistro. I prefer Italian. In fact, I don't like French food all that much. But he seemed excited and said, "French food is my favorite. Well . . . that and Indian food. I love Indian food." Then he told me the best Indian food he ever ate was in a restaurant in Cape Town, South Africa. Who knew?

We entered through a screened door that opened to a long, narrow porch with plants. It was 97 degrees outside, so we sat inside with air-conditioning. The place was quaint. We took a seat in a high-arc wooden booth and ordered steak frites.

He ordered medium rare.

I like mine well-done. Burnt.

We enjoyed a lovely bottle of Grgich Hills Cabernet on the side.

Topping off our feast was a crème brûlée to share.

Big Johnson shared stories of his college days. "I stocked shelves in a grocery store during the graveyard shift to put myself through law school," he said. "Stocking grocery shelves and playing pool."

I put my spoon down and looked at him. "Playing pool?"

"Yeah, it paid for law books while keeping me watered and fed in the French Quarter."

From the first time I'd played pool in a sleazy bar at eighteen, I'd imagined I could someday become a pool hustler—later in life, like when I was sixty-five. I'd always thought it would be the perfect second career. And since I'd be waiting till my sixties, I'd have a lifetime to learn. No one would suspect an old lady clearing the table. And it would be the only table I would ever want to clear. There was something sexy about pool. It's all geometry and physics. Angles and motion. I just needed to learn how to hit the ball in the right spot with the right amount of action.

"Wanna play?" he asked.

"Now?"

"Yeah."

Big Johnson drove two blocks down Ventura Boulevard and parked in front of JJ Sullivan's. When he held the door open for me, I could already tell there would be no Napa Cabs served here. Beer on tap, wine in a jug, and hard liquor only. A mammoth bar stood in the center of the room. Narrow aisles lined both sides between the barstools and the walls. Aerosmith's "Walk This Way" blared from the jukebox. Big Johnson took my hand and led the way toward the back of the bar where a lone, well-worn pool table stood.

He grabbed a pool stick from the rack on the wall and rolled it across the table, checking to see if the stick had warped. After approving its competence, he chalked up the tip and handed it to me. He did the same for himself before racking the table, making sure the solids and stripes were evenly distributed within the triangle.

"Ladies first?" he offered.

I shook my head. "I don't want to break. That's the hardest part."

With the ease and precision of a professional, he placed the cue ball on the table, pulled back his stick, and ran the table until it was a block shot on the eight ball. Then, pool shark that he was, he pulled the bridge off the wall, lined it up with the pool cue tip low to the cue ball, jumped my ball, and hit the eight ball into the side pocket, showing me he could put a ball anywhere, and also give the game to me.

Who was this man?

Peter Pan

WHILE RESEARCHING IN the present the men of my past, I realize that more than half of them never had children. Was that because they had never grown up themselves? Having lived in their own Neverland? Since I was attracted to them, they were mirroring back to me who I was: Patty Pan.

Keys to the Kingdom

ONE MORNING, BACK at Big Johnson Winery after our pool playing adventure while enjoying my morning latte and cinnamon roll, Big Johnson handed me a key to the house.

"I want you to be able to come and go."

I looked at the key in the palm of my hand.

"Enjoy yourself here. I'm happy when you're here. How about we go out and purchase some fancy sheets? Like what we slept on up north while wine tasting."

"I love fine linens. Do you like percale or sateen? Percale is my favorite, but I also like sleeping on linen."

Big Johnson leaned down to kiss me, interrupting my enthusiastic obsession with sheets.

"Whatever makes you happy," he said before he left the room.

A man who appreciates good bed linens is sexy.

Dirty Laundry

"LET'S MAKE A quick trip to Santa Ynez and check out their vineyards since they're closer than Napa," Big Johnson announced.

So we jumped in the car and headed north. We stopped at vineyard after vineyard, sampling delicious wines and foods along the way. We had so much fun we decided to stay a few extra days, but we'd run out of clean clothes.

"Back in my navy JAG days, I'd wash my uniform in the toilet. The trick, after cleaning the toilet bowl, is four flushes, not three, and make sure you get a good grip on the sleeve so you don't lose your shirt during one of the flush cycles."

Disgusted yet captivated by such a creative idea, I wanted to know more.

"And how did you press them?"

"Sat on them."

Big Johnson, pondering our predicament, then suggested, "If you don't like the toilet bowl idea, we could put on all our dirty clothes and run through the water fountain on the square."

Thinking I'd rather shower with all my clothes on than partake in a public washing, I came up with other possible solutions for our dressing dilemma, like wearing our clothes inside out.

Finally, Big Johnson made another announcement.

"Let's send the laundry out."

And that's when I officially fell in love with him.

Meet the Girls

AS SOON AS Big Johnson's daughters returned from Barcelona, he set up a meet and greet.

I knew his girls would love Ron Howard. Everyone loved Ron Howard. So at least I had that going for me.

Big Johnson entertained us at Bobby's Rib Joint. He sat next to me on one side of the booth so I'd be able to enjoy the girls from across the table. The eldest, in braces and glasses, had just turned twelve. She was fearless and as vibrant as a sunset in Hawaii. The youngest, freckled in her pageboy haircut, was more reserved than her older sister while smart beyond her ten years. They entertained us with their travels in Spain and talked nonstop about all the tapas they ate.

After we returned to the vineyard, just as Ron and I were getting into my car to go home, the girls stood in the driveway, and the oldest pleaded, "Can you stay?"

The youngest looked at her dad and said, "Can she stay, please?"

I looked at Big Johnson. "Well, you do have a guest room." I grinned at all three of them.

"Yes, and it's got a television in it," the eldest said to entice me. "What kind of shows do you like?"

"I like yellow-tape shows."

The youngest tilted her head as she furrowed her brow. "What's a yellow-tape show?"

"Well, there's usually a scene where a police officer yellow tapes off an area where something bad happened, marking it as a crime scene, and someone needs to solve the crime. It's almost always some sort of police or detective show."

Back inside, Big Johnson wasn't ready to let the girls watch a yellow-tape show, and I didn't know a single Disney show, so we settled on playing Wii. The youngest won all the games. Her specialty—*Mario Kart*. I wanted to hire her to be my chauffeur, but she was only ten. We took on *Wii Fit* next, where she was also the fittest. I won the meditation event, where all I had to do was sit still the longest.

When I entered the guest room for the first time that evening, the girls had left me a note with instructions to turn on the television and where I could find all the *Law & Order* I wanted.

A Gift from the Girls

THE NEXT MORNING before breakfast, the girls gathered Big Johnson, Ron Howard, and me in the living room and sang a song they wrote.

Lisa and Ron Howard her dog
Are the sunshine in the thick fog
No matter the weather
Lisa will smile
While Ron Howard walks a mile
We can't wait to see you again.

Double Take

"BY THE AUTHORITY vested in me by the State of California, I now pronounce you husband and wife." I heard the words, but all I saw was my husband.

Big Johnson leaned down and kissed me.

Nervousness and excitement fluttered through my body. *I did it. I really did! I'm married now.*

Big Johnson took my hand as we walked back up the aisle. Guests blew bubbles as they gathered around us. I waved to friends and family with one hand and placed my other hand over my heart. It was beating so strong with happiness and love for those who had come to celebrate with us. Such a magical moment. As I scanned our loved ones, I landed on my dance teacher alongside my goddaughter smiling as they checked each other out. They were wearing the same dress. The exact same Lilly Pulitzer dress.

Another Invite

THE FOLLOWING WEEK, when the girls were with Big Johnson, we all sat around the dining room table, devouring our Denny's takeout of pancakes, eggs, sausage, and bacon. The girls began discussing their upcoming trip to Texas and Virginia.

Every summer Big Johnson and his girls spent time with his family: his brother in Texas and his parents in Virginia. While discussing their list of activities—horseback riding, renting a powerboat, and zip-lining—the youngest, chewing on a sausage link, looked at me and said, "You're coming with us, right?"

"Uh . . . I hadn't planned to." I smiled a huge grin, feeling so honored to be included.

"You should come. We're gonna have fun," the eldest followed up.

Big Johnson took a sip of his Diet Pepsi and said, "Why don't you join us?"

A Visit with the Brother

BIG JOHNSON'S BROTHER was his elder brother. He wasn't nearly as big, and he was certainly more soft-spoken. So much so that we barely spoke.

The brother drove us to a ranch where we went horseback riding, something I hadn't done since I was fourteen. Unless you count my donkey ride down the mountain in Yunnan, China, but I really didn't. This morning trail ride was only an hour, but it felt like days. After I dismounted, I walked like a cowboy for the rest of my stay.

The next afternoon we pigged out on ribs in a saloon with a dance floor the size of a football field. One rode horses during the day here and danced the two-step at night. We shopped at a store called Gypsy Cowgirl, where the youngest bought a shawl. There was even a trip to an obstacle course, complete with a high wire. I nursed my equestrian wounds from the sidelines.

Big Johnson bought me a round-trip ticket to Texas, but his girls convinced their dad, again, that I needed to extend my trip to join them in Virginia Beach. And before I knew it, I was on a plane to meet the parents.

Meeting the Johnsons

FROM THE MOMENT we entered their home, enthusiasm and excitement became the air we breathed. Both parents a young ninety-three years old, I found their effervescence for life inspiring. Shirley followed the news twenty-four seven, read all the gossip magazines, and played in her treasure chest of jewelry she'd acquired on their vacations to Hong Kong. After fondling a piece and admiring its beauty, she insisted we modeled each trinket for her while she laid in bed in awe.

Johnny, completely bedbound, needed to hear from the girls all about their summer.

Life was big with Big Johnson, nonstop activities. First, he rented a boat. Motored it through the causeways and out on the Atlantic Ocean. Then, from the grandparents' backyard, Big Johnson taught the girls how to fish. We ate pizza that night. We even spent a day at the beach under a cabana. Big Johnson and his girls swam in the ocean. I read, taking full advantage of our hut on the beach.

Though we were only there a few days, every moment felt larger than life. Every moment packed with fun. When we turned in for the evening, we shared with his parents about our days while they marveled at all we'd accomplished.

Never a dull moment with the Johnsons.

The Naked Truth

WHILE IN VIRGINIA Beach, Big Johnson not only entertained his girls but also did his best to show me the town.

Breakfast was served at Hardee's. Yes, the fast-food chain that's from North Carolina where my family is from. They're known for their baked-from-scratch biscuits. Hot and flaky right out of the oven. My favorite is the country ham biscuit.

Dinner was at Creekside, walking distance from Johnny and Shirley's house, where they had the best she-crab soup, according to Big Johnson, who was not only an expert on lobster bisque but also prided himself on being a virtuoso on she-crab soup.

After we put the girls and parents to bed our last night there, Big Johnson grinned.

"I wanna take you to the beach."

"Now? It's midnight."

"That's why I wanna take you."

We hopped into our rental car and drove to a small beach on the inlet just off the causeway from his parents' house. A full moon filled the sky, glistening on the waves as they rolled in. Low tide provided a wide beach to walk on.

"Come on, let's take a dip."

"I didn't bring a bathing suit."

"We're going skinny-dipping." He stripped off his T-shirt and unzipped his jeans.

"No, we're not! Not on a public beach!" My heart raced at the thought of being naked in public. "There's a ten-story hotel just over there." I pointed to a high-rise one hundred feet away.

"They're all asleep. Nobody cares."

"I do."

"Well, I'm going in," he announced as his boxer shorts hit the sand. Off he ran toward the ocean's edge. All three hundred pounds of him waded into the water. In his birthday suit. He was so uninhibited and unencumbered. Diving in like a pelican, dancing like a dolphin, and playing like a sea otter, Big Johnson was living his best life.

I want to spend every moment with this man.

Something Old

AFTER SKINNY-DIPPING in the Atlantic, we crawled into bed.

Big Johnson whispered, "What kind of engagement ring would you like?"

"I don't want anything new. Would you ask Shirley for something of hers that she doesn't wear? Maybe something in the back of her jewelry box?"

"Really? You don't want something new?"

"Nope. I want something from your family. It would mean so much more."

"Okay. I'm glad we had this talk," Big Johnson said before he kissed me good night.

Card Shark

BIG JOHNSON LOVED Vegas.

I never liked Vegas, but he wanted to show me why he loved it, his Vegas. So I thought, *It's only forty-eight hours. I can do forty-eight hours. At least I think I can.*

He'd booked the Mandarin Oriental, which is on the Strip, but the entrance was so elusive you'd miss it if you didn't turn right behind the liquor store with a quick left to open a nondescript door.

Upon entrance, there wasn't a casino, just an elevator that went up to the lobby. It was silent, as in no Muzak in the elevator, providing the air of an exclusive club. Free from the clanging and banging of slot machines, screams from craps tables, and all the bachelorette broods stumbling their way to their next watering hole.

Our fifteenth-floor room not only came with floor-to-ceiling windows overlooking the Strip but also fluffy white robes and a tub so massive I never wanted to leave.

It turned out, Big Johnson's a player.

A blackjack player.

And I was given an up close and private observation of the player in his playground. His own personal Las Vegas.

He'd scout a table and take a seat where the energy moved him. He'd play several winning hands, collecting chips in all colors, until the energy moved him to another table. He'd advise me when to take a card and when to stay.

So much to learn. When to hold at seventeen and take a hit when the dealer is probably holding a face card. Later, after cashing out all our chips, we dined at a fancy steak house, where he told me stories of all his previous winning weekends.

We took our time holding hands as we meandered around the blackjack areas in various casinos, stopping at tables Big Johnson sensed victorious, collecting more chips along the way.

By the end of the weekend, he'd paid for our entire road trip with his winnings.

I respect a good card player. Especially one who walks away ahead.

The Band

BEFORE WE LEFT Vegas, Big Johnson took my hand and said, "So, we haven't spent all my winnings, and I think it's always better to leave them here, in Vegas. Spend it where you make it, and then it will be here when we come back again."

What girl doesn't want to hear that?

And with that, he took me to pick out my sparkling diamond wedding band, leaving all his extra winnings at Tiffany's.

The Proposal

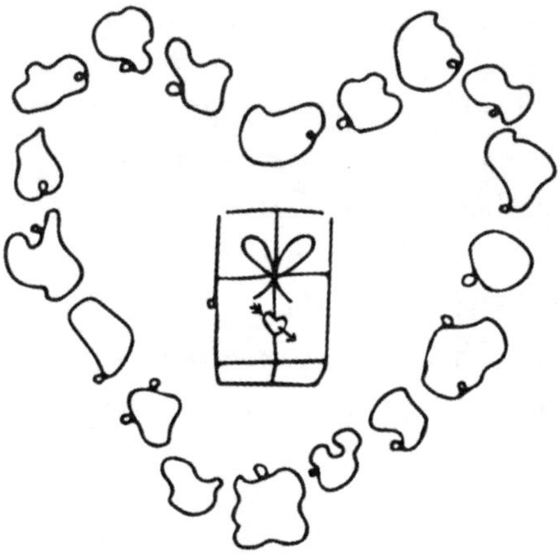

IT WAS AN overcast Sunday morning, my favorite kind of day in LA, when I hopped into my silver VW Bug and headed down Ventura Boulevard. I'm not the kind of girl who gets her nails done, but something told me tonight was the night Big Johnson was going to propose.

Besides, after we'd had that conversation in Virginia about his mother's ring, he'd let it slip, "I've made a dinner reservation at Morton's tonight 'cause we got something to celebrate." By now, I'd discovered that Big Johnson was not the best at keeping secrets, so I wanted my hands to look their best.

As the exit ramp from the 101 merged with the boulevard traffic, a white Toyota Camry cut into my lane and slammed on its brakes. As I stomped on mine and came to a stop, a red

BMW rear-ended me, causing my VW Beetle to crash into the bumper of the Camry.

The airbag deployed and punched me in the face—hard. Feeling my face beginning to swell, I reached for my cell phone and called Big Johnson. He was on his way downtown, but immediately turned around, picked me up at the scene of the accident, and drove me to the hospital.

♡

We returned from the emergency room with my arm in a sling and bruises everywhere. No broken bones. My fingernails still naked and jagged.

"Come on," Big Johnson suggested. "Let's go upstairs and lie down for a while." He held my hand as we walked up the staircase, one step at a time. At the top, we stepped through the French doors that led to the bedroom. In the middle of the king-size sleigh bed was a large heart made out of red rose petals. In the center of the rose-petal heart lay a hot pink watch-shaped box. The top of the box read "BETSEY JOHNSON," with "BETSEY" crossed out in black Sharpie and "LISA" written over it. Just below that, he'd written, "I heart you!" Above my name was a hand-drawn heart with an arrow through it. He'd inscribed "C.J. + L.C." in the middle of the heart.

Inside the box was an antique platinum diamond ring he'd received from his mom.

Big Johnson lumbered down on one knee as he reached for my hand and said, "I promise to always take care of you. To love and adore you. Will you marry me?"

I looked at this big hunk of a man and said, "I can't wait!"

The Celebration Dinner

AFTER A FIVE-HOUR flight across the country and an hour drive from the airport, we arrived at my father's house at sunset. In anticipation of our arrival, Dad had chilled a couple bottles of sparkling wine. My sister and her husband lived nearby and dropped in to celebrate. The five of us circled up on the terra-cotta linoleum floor, surrounded by walnut cabinets. Every countertop and table overflowed with hot sauce, steak sauce, generic orange soda, Diet Pepsi, champagne, and ginger ale shoved long ways against the wine rack. A box wine rack for three—one red, one white, and the third whatever had been on sale at the time of purchase. No one wanted to drink Dad's bargain box of wine.

Waiting for someone to say something, Big Johnson raised his glass. "Do I have your blessing, sir, to marry your daughter?"

"We've been waiting a very long time for this day." Dad snickered, raising his flute as he smiled at both of us. "Yes, you do, and congratulations on your upcoming nuptials."

My sister and her husband held up their glasses. My sister's feet moved back and forth underneath her as if she had somewhere else to be. Eau de Impatience emitted from her body, a fake smile frozen on her face.

Glasses clinked, and the bottle of bubbly was consumed.

Dad was dressed in his five dollar Ghana T-shirt purchased on our cruise up the west coast of Africa. His stylish dungarees hung below his belly because his waist had outgrown the circumference of his Kmart blue jeans. His beautiful blue eyes, the color of morning glories, had been wide open in anticipation of this entire day, now wilted. It was five thirty in the afternoon, and I knew he'd be in bed asleep before eight.

He put his arm around my shoulders and squeezed my body sideways, smiling a grin the size of any of the quokkas you see on social media. "He's a great guy. I'm really happy for you. Gonna put the steaks on the grill. You hungry?"

"Am I ever. Thanks, Dad."

He grabbed the platter of steaks, marinating in a special sauce he'd concocted, from the top of the stove since there was no room on the countertops. While scooping up a pair of tongs and his glass of bubbly, he asked, "How does Big Johnson like his steak?"

"Rare," I said.

"He's my kind of guy."

♡

Dinner was served in the formal dining room. My grandmother's floor-to-ceiling china cabinet stood in the corner, chock-full of mismatched china and other fancy pieces that were no longer used. Across from the china cabinet, Dad's cherished bar was overstocked with liquors, aperitifs, and bottles of wine. Butter and sour cream for the baked potatos, Heinz 57, HP, and A.1. moved across the table like a game of Chinese checkers. We drank from bottomless wine boxes while no one touched their iceberg lettuce salad.

"So, how's life at the vineyard?" Dad asked.

"Just planted another twenty-five vines, and we'll have our first harvest in about a month. It all depends on the sugar levels."

"They have to read a certain amount of sugar before it's ready for fermentation, right?" Dad asked, topping off everyone's glass of red. He'd toured enough wineries to drop the lingo of wine making, but his real passion was consuming it.

"Yeah. You want to come pick them when they're ready?" Big Johnson asked.

"No thanks. I'm gonna leave that to you two. But if you need help drinking it, I'm your man."

All of a sudden, a wave of exhaustion hit me. Maybe from the stress of introducing everyone and now it was done? My whole body ached from the car accident, and the bruising on my arms and ribs along with my sprained wrist hurt. And I'm sure spending the day traveling through airports didn't help.

I couldn't wait for Big Johnson to meet my family. My sister and her husband had been living abroad for years and had recently rented a place near my father. At some point, the conversation turned to American politics. My sister, while pouring herself yet another glass of wine, shouted, apropos of nothing, "I'm tired of my tax dollars paying for wars! This country spends all its money on destroying the rest of the world. I hate that my brother flies in and out of war zones all the time."

Our half brother, a pilot in the air force, had been stationed in the Middle East, moving troops and supplies in and out of Afghanistan. He couldn't make the dinner tonight even though he currently lived an hour from my dad—and now I wished he were here to take her on.

But more to the point, why were we talking politics when I'd finally snagged a husband? I'd finally found a man I was willing to do time with, and she was poking the bear. I looked at her and said, "Our brother knew what he was signing up for when he entered the air force."

"I know I did when I signed up," Big Johnson chimed in. I could tell he was bewildered by where the conversation had gone; we'd all had too much to drink. And it was also clear to me that she was super wound up, for reasons I wasn't ever going to know.

“Me too,” Dad said, evoking his time as a commander in the navy. “It’s an honor to serve this country.”

There was an edge in my sister’s voice. *So disrespectful*, I thought—to my husband-to-be and to Dad and our brother. I was pissed. Where was this coming from? Why was she behaving like this? I jumped in to support my loved ones.

“When was the last time you paid taxes in this country, anyway?” I asked. “You’ve been living across the pond for over a decade.”

“Well, you know.” She quivered as she stared at me. Her peridot eyes so hard, they could cut diamonds. “If I were living here . . .” she huffed. All eyes were on her as she finally trailed off, appearing to have nothing left to say.

All I wanted was for my sister to like my husband-to-be. I wanted her to be happy for me.

I had expectations.

For as long as I can remember, I was the people pleaser in my family.

When I was eight, my father was transferred back to the States after an overseas posting. I was sent to live with my father’s parents in Chapel Hill, where I would attend the first part of third grade while my parents were “finding a house” in Detroit, a place my mother was very unhappy about living in.

The week of Christmas, I traveled to move in with my parents. Then on Christmas morning after unwrapping our gifts, my parents announced they were getting a divorce. They handed me a piece of paper and a No. 2 pencil and told me to go to my room and make a decision for both my sister and me as to who we’d live with. I was responsible for all of us. I needed to please everyone in my family.

My parents didn’t know that Grandma Cheek had already prepped me a month earlier, telling me that if my parents got a divorce, I was to choose to live with my father. While living overseas, my mother almost died after giving birth to my baby sister, born three months early. My mom was so sick my sister came home six weeks before Mom did. Mom was overwhelmed and probably suffered from postpartum depression, too.

At age eight, I understood she could not take care of me. Having left Dad once before when I was five, she really tried to be on her own with me, but it just wasn't in the cards. So we went back to my dad after he promised Mom a transfer out of the country, but ultimately it didn't save their marriage.

As soon as I got to Detroit, I could see my mother was so unhappy and unable to take care of a baby and her older daughter at the same time.

I had to be the adult in the family. And that's how I became a people pleaser. A family pleaser. My role was to keep peace and make everyone happy. I hadn't yet learned that I wasn't responsible for everyone's happiness. But I did make the choice for my sister and me to live with my dad, and that meant I was responsible for my sister's and my mother's happiness. My sister and I had been through so much together, with a mother living so far away, and being so young, I took on the role of taking care of her. Then there were stepmothers and blended families that weren't the best decisions, but I didn't make those. They happened to us. I loved my sister with all my heart, and from the time she was born, I wanted her to be happy. But it wasn't my job to make people happy anymore. I needed to make myself happy.

The Ride

"COME ON," BIG Johnson said as he took my hand and led me, with Ron Howard at my side, down the walkway to an unattended golf cart that sat in the driveway. Simply Red played through the speakers, singing "Turn It Up," as our guests mingled, dining on the mushroom and cheese tarts.

Big Johnson escorted me to the passenger side and helped me make sure my dress and veil were all tucked inside before he placed Ron Howard on my lap. I moved my legs around until Ron Howard's little black nose, eyes, and blond, wispy pointed ears peeked just above the windshield so he could enjoy our unplanned adventure. Big Johnson jumped into the driver's seat and looked over at me.

"We're going for a ride." He flashed a huge grin at me and drove down the driveway.

My whole body filled with joy at the freedom I'd just experienced. It never occurred to me to take these quirky transportation vehicles we'd hired for our wedding guests for a spin ourselves. But it had occurred to Big Johnson. He was always looking for a moment of fun.

I had no idea where we were headed, but I liked where we were going.

I Heard It Through the Grapevine

I HEARD THIS from a reliable source who wishes to remain anonymous, so I'm gonna do my best to accurately recount what I was told, but remember—it's all hearsay.

Later in the evening, before cake cutting and long after all the toasts, most of the guests had joined the dance floor, dancing to The Spinners' "I'll Be Around." Feeling no pain and enjoying his buzz, Dad danced with my sister. His eyes closed, he had a big smile plastered on his face.

That was when my mother chose to cut in. Dad swayed back and forth, none the wiser. When he finally opened his eyes, he blinked several times, not sure whether to steady himself from all the wine he'd consumed or because he couldn't believe what he was looking at. Last time he'd been looking, he'd been dancing with his beloved daughter—and now he was face-to-face with his first wife. The wife he detested most! He pursed his lips while grinding his teeth and glared a hard stare at my mom for the briefest of moments. Then he dashed off the dance floor, leaving my mother laughing and thinking she'd pulled one over on him again.

In Dad's defense, my mom and my sister do look alike.

No wonder I wasn't in a rush to get married.

Seeing Red

WHENEVER MY FATHER didn't like clothes or decorations I'd picked out, he'd say, "Your taste is in your mouth." Like I knew nothing about how to put together an outfit or a room.

Living with Big Johnson meant moving into his McMansion, which meant intermingling our personal styles and tastes. The downstairs living area consisted of a stadium-sized, suede, lemon-chiffon-colored pullout sectional sofa that he'd complemented with an olive-green-and-black marble coffee table the size of a small country. In the dining room, he'd hung crimson-red curtains that he'd creatively partnered with eight coral-red dining room chairs. Upstairs, in the primary bedroom and bath, he'd installed four ruby-red blinds that had been paired with five candy-apple-red bath mats and six large scarlet-red bath towels.

Big Johnson even drove a Lexus RX350 in Matador Red.

Red was everywhere.

When I inquired about his decorating color of choice, Big Johnson's reply was, "I like red."

"But it looks like we live in a bordello."

"Is that a bad thing?" he asked, followed by a huge grin.

I like the color red, too, but think it's best when one is wearing it. A lipstick, a pair of shoes, or a smart handbag is the best place for the vibrant and alive color, certainly not splashed across every surface where one eats and sleeps.

Even though I hadn't always dreamed of getting married, I had somehow imagined that if I shared my life with someone, it would be in a minimalist, all-white modern house, like the ones I'd seen on television shows. I wanted a grown-up home. A quiet, peaceful place to relax in. Not some old-timey cathouse that belonged in a vintage Western film.

As soon as we'd spent enough time together, the ruby-red blinds and extra-large scarlet-red bath sheets moved down by the work sink in the garage where we gave Ron Howard his baths. I made peace with the eight terra-cotta-red dining room chairs. Turns out they're quite comfortable, and they do hide the penne arrabbiata and barbecue pork rib stains, so I guess my father was right: My taste is in my mouth, and now on my dining room chairs.

Goldilocks

MY POSSESSIONS ARRIVED via professional movers one Saturday afternoon. All of my furniture had been in storage due to selling my home and spending the past two years working and traveling. Most of my furniture I'd inherited from my English grandmother, so it consisted of antiques.

Since Big Johnson's house was already fully furnished, we put my treasures in his six-car garage to sort out later. I couldn't wait to be surrounded by some of "my things" again. I wanted to use my two-hundred-year-old dining room table and chairs, but when Big Johnson took a seat in one of them, the legs wobbled and his butt hung over the sides. Then, when he tried to slip the rickety chair under the table, his knees and lap were too tall to sit under it.

My slipper chairs, narrow and low to the ground, Big Johnson didn't even attempt to sit in because he knew he'd never be able to get out.

In my queen-size bed, his feet hung off the end. He was so tall, only his California king would do.

I'd have to learn the art of compromise and let go of my stuff in order to live with Big Johnson. It hurt at first, but as each day came and went, life with him meant so much more to me than that old junk.

Things

MERGING ONE'S LIVES means merging one's belongings. Having had two homes before we married, we now also had two toasters, too many televisions, and *way* too many tape measures, and yet we could never find one when we needed it.

So, I started to consolidate our stuff.

After sorting through seven large plastic bins of Big Johnson's PVC pipes; five overstuffed containers of electrical wires, plugs, tape, and outlet covers; six redundantly filled toolboxes; and four boxes of outdated computer cables, I wondered, *Why does he have all this crap?* Really, if there were a plumbing problem, call a plumber! Electrical? Call an electrician! How many toolboxes can one person cart around?

Yes, I have more dresses than I want to admit, but one day I might just fit into all of them.

I emerged from the garage one day with two pressing questions: "Why do we need ten-year-old sporting equipment that's never been used?" and "Exactly how many ladders does it take to change a light bulb?"

Big Johnson retorted with his own question: "Why do you have all these plastic bags?"

Truth was, I'd been collecting plastic bags for eight years, ever since Ron Howard came to live with me. I knew the day would come when there would be no more "free" plastic bags—and I was going to be prepared! So, I'd started organizing my plastic bag collection, putting them in their appropriate containers.

I realized that Big Johnson was right. I really did have a plastic bag problem. I was a plastic bag addict.

I decided not to question Big Johnson about his two-by-four collection leaning against the garage door or the twenty paint rollers shoved in the overstuffed cubbyholes in the storage area. That way Ron Howard could live to be one hundred and I'd never have to pay out of pocket for his poop bags.

BTW, it takes seven ladders to change a light bulb in our household, or at least that's how many we have.

Blended Family

BIG JOHNSON IS a cat person.

I am a dog person.

He has two big male cats named Paws and Whiskers.

I have one little adorable furry best friend, Ron Howard, who's not only cute but smart.

Big Johnson never disclosed exactly where he rescued "the Brothers" from, but I secretly think they were from a seedy suburb of LA before he brought them to the Valley.

The Brothers are tight, and not just because they're blood related, but because they seem to have formed their own kitty gang, which from my point of view resembles the Crips, the Bloods, and the Hells Angels all in one. I haven't actually seen them cruising on Harleys or packing heat, but I have witnessed them more than once sharpening their claws at 4 a.m. on our one-thousand-thread-count Egyptian cotton sheets.

Ron Howard has attended many training schools, including acting. He knows how to go to his mark on a set, to "high-five," and to "touch product." One month, he even paid the mortgage starring in a Pedigree commercial.

The Brothers don't seem to find Mr. Adorable so adorable. Perhaps they think he's taking over their territory? Or maybe he's going through some kind of initiation? The thing is when the Brothers do strike, Mr. Adorable doesn't have a chance. Big Johnson will be representing the Brothers, clearing them of all oppressed charges that might be brought against them.

Must-See TV

MY FAVORITE SHOWS: *Modern Family*, *The Good Wife*, and *The Office*.

Big Johnson's favorite shows: *Modern Sniper*, *Greatest Tank Battles*, and *Ultimate Weapons*.

I'm glad we never got around to consolidating our televisions.

TCB (Taking Care of Business)

EVERY DAY, THREE to four times a day, Ron Howard and I perused our neighborhood. It was our time together when it was all about us moseying around our surroundings. Investigating what was new, what was gone, or what had stayed the same. Like the blossoms appearing on jacaranda trees, or the junk a neighbor had dumped on the curb for someone to take and use in their home, or the fire hydrant, aka the bulletin board for dogs, which Ron Howard liked to stop by to gather the report of who had checked in that day. This was a time for Ron and me to roam together.

Santa Monica is a small town by the beach where people live in apartments, condos, and duplexes with shops and restaurants just a block or two away. Ron and I liked the hustle and bustle of people picking up coffee and bagels while neighbors jogged and walked their dogs.

Our mornings in Santa Monica held such promise. Just me and Ron Howard. While he took care of his business, I contemplated my day.

After we moved to Big Johnson Winery, our walks changed. We were a mile south of Ventura Boulevard on a hilly and twisty road. The neighborhood contained single-family dwellings with large yards and no sidewalks. Not even center white lines painted down the middle of the tarred streets, so our ritual looked different. It was a quiet neighborhood. The stillness of each morning accentuated the bird chatter while the soft morning light highlighted the dew on the grass.

Also, now Big Johnson accompanied us. I brought plastic bags, while Big Johnson came prepared with a cigar and a can of Diet Pepsi. The three of us moved through the neighborhood like a float in the Rose Bowl Parade—a middle-aged woman walking her small fluffy dog accompanied by a large man smoking a cigar enjoying his Diet Pepsi, before breakfast, waving to our neighbors.

One morning, I rolled over in bed to find Big Johnson and Ron Howard missing. I panicked, thinking Big Johnson was downstairs feeding Ron rib eye for breakfast. He really wanted to win Ron Howard over—always slipping that canine something delicious, and there was nothing I could do about it, because it not only made Big Johnson happy but Ron Howard too.

But there was no noise from the kitchen, so I jumped out of bed. Not a sign of them anywhere. I checked the office and the garage, eventually running to the porch and peering out over the grapevines, where I caught a glimpse of Ron Howard's tail wagging while smoke trailed behind them. They'd let me sleep in and were having their own adventure. It made my heart melt. My two guys, having a morning romp around the vineyard together.

I hope Ron's outings helped him walk off all the extra treats.

A Gift for the Guests

THE MONTH AFTER I moved in with Big Johnson, the vineyard produced its first harvest. Seventy-five bottles of Big Johnson Cabernet.

I'd designed the logo for Big Johnson Winery, but we didn't have a label for the bottles we'd be giving to our wedding guests. Together, we researched where we might get one. Nothing sparked us, so I gave up and decided we'd go with personalized wineglasses instead.

An hour before our rehearsal dinner, Big Johnson ran in.

"I got labels!" he shouted with enthusiasm, handing over a bottle of wine for me to examine.

Below my logo was our wedding invitation. It was perfect.

My heart jumped.

The most romantic gesture ever.

Hooking Up

AT SOME POINT in the evening, I lost Ron Howard.

I checked the kitchen, where I felt sure he'd be begging for nibbles. Everywhere, someone was always feeding him.

Since the lamb lollipops were receiving great reviews, I figured Ron was on the hunt. I checked the upstairs patio to see if a party guest had been sharing their lamb chops with him.

I even tried the hors d'oeuvre table.

Finally, I scoured the outskirts of the vineyard, climbing the wide staircase built from railway ties. There, I heard a rustling of leaves. Thinking I'd found him, I moved closer, but it wasn't Ron Howard. I'd stumbled upon Frankie and my handsome, single friend Joe in a full-on embrace, swapping spit.

"Oops," I said. "I'm looking for Ron."

They both giggled, and then Frankie said, "I haven't seen him, but I haven't been looking for him either." Followed by another giggle.

Just then, Ron sprinted from the other side of the vineyard, and we both ran back down to the patio where the party continued.

I Heart You

TEN MINUTES LATER, Frankie descended from the top of the vineyard, grinning while fluffing up her hair. I watched her cross the patio, stopping to blow a few bubbles with a five-year-old guest, who chuckled while they watched the bubbles float up among the grapevines. When a server offered her something from her tray, Frankie grabbed it, took a bite, and made a beeline over my way.

"You need to eat!" Frankie insisted as she handed me her half-eaten lamb lollipop. "I'll get you a fresh one. And some tri-tip. It's yummy. Stay here by the patio door so I can find you."

Bill Withers's "Lovely Day" was up on the playlist. I watched a couple who'd flown in from the East Coast. They'd been together for over thirty years, and they smiled as they sang to each other while they danced. They'd had a commitment ceremony ten years before since same-sex marriage wasn't legal, but that didn't stop them from living each day side by side for the past three decades.

Ron Howard chased bubbles the five-year-old blew while dancing in a circle.

I pulled at my ponytail, trying to place it higher on my head, knowing that if it hit the right spot on the back of my head, I looked younger. With my neck stretching down and looking at the patio we'd laid a month earlier for the wedding, I spotted a heart etched into the cement by Big Johnson. He'd drawn it right by the door, as if to say, *There's love in this house*. I'd only noticed it because we'd moved the welcome mats for the party.

Big Johnson was big on leaving hearts for me to find. I'd never met a man who loved hearts the way he did. It was as if he was leaving me love notes. I'd look in the full-length mirror by the front door and spot a red heart sticker staring back at me. He'd put a sticker on my computer screen before he'd leave for work. He'd drop off takeout with hearts he'd drawn all over the box. Hearts were his thing. And he melted my heart.

Big Johnson is all heart.

The Ring

"SHIRLEY WANTS TO speak to you." Big Johnson handed me his iPhone, a dollop of ketchup from the slider he'd just stuffed into his mouth clinging to the side by the volume button.

"Hi, Shirley."

"Welcome to the family," she said. "You're officially a Johnson now." Big Johnson wrapped his arm around my waist and looked out onto the dance floor while I held the phone tight to my ear, trying to hear her over Bruno Mars as everyone danced to "Marry You."

"How does it feel? I know my son loves you very much."

I didn't feel different at all. Just stressed. And I wasn't ready to tell my not-yet-mother-in-law that we weren't really married. The guests had now formed a conga line and were dancing through the vineyard.

"We're having such a great time. Wish you were here."

"Well, I won't keep you from your party, but I wanted you to know that I wore that diamond on my hand for sixty-two years. When my son asked me for a ring for you, I didn't hesitate. I took it off my hand and handed it to him. Jasmine Johnson, the Colonel's mother, wore it before me for forty-one years. Over one hundred years of Johnson women have worn it every day. And now, all the joy we have had in our marriages is passed on to you."

I looked down at the sparkly emerald-cut antique ring twinkling in the light. I'd asked for a ring at the back of her jewelry box. Something she never wore. Something she didn't want. But no, that's not what I got. Shirley had turned over to me her most treasured gift: a symbol of love and family. And she gave it freely, wanting that same love and happiness for her son.

Having had no idea of what was wrapped around my finger, I exhaled the biggest breath. "Thank you for sharing that with me."

Big Johnson reached for another slider as the waitress walked by, splitting his mini burger with Ron Howard. Ron licked his lips waiting for more, knowing Big Johnson would find another bite for him.

"I love that you are my daughter. Now go dance the night away."

Let's Get It On

BIG JOHNSON WIPED the crumbs from his chin before he pulled out a container of bubbles from his coat pocket and blew them around the two of us—creating the most magical moment.

"Come on, I found someone to marry us."

"What?" I asked, still mulling over what Shirley had just shared with me. "Who?"

"Harvey. He's a state judge. He can marry us! He asked if he could officiate our wedding but I'd already asked Mike. Harvey and his girlfriend are waiting on the front balcony to marry us."

"Now?"

"Now."

How crazy was it that there was someone here to marry us?

Here was my chance at a do-over.

An opportunity to say "I do" again.

To do it with a new realization. After spending my wedding reception examining my family dynamics, I realized none of them cared if their family approved of the mate they were going to marry. If they did, they went ahead and married anyway, knowing that their person was who made them happy. They weren't trying to make anyone happy but themselves. And I do know that happiness is an inside job. It's not my job anymore to make other people happy or prove to them this is a good decision. This is about Big Johnson and me. And no one has ever been as much fun to be around or loved me more.

I thought about how my sister had married who she'd wanted to and didn't care what anyone thought. I thought about how my mom had left us for London, for her own happiness. I thought about how happy Big Johnson made me feel. How every day was an adventure with him. And what an honor and a privilege it had been to share each day with him so far.

While Barry White's "You're the First, the Last, My Everything" echoed from the dance floor, I took a seat at an empty high-top and made a quick list.

PROS

1. He's handsome.
2. He's kind.
3. He sees me.
4. He loves me for me.
5. He loves Ron Howard.
6. He's trustworthy.
7. He's adventurous.
8. He's funny on occasion.
9. He's generous.
10. He's thoughtful.
11. He's comfortable with himself.
12. He's confident.
13. He's smart.
14. He's fun.
15. He's supportive.
16. He loves his parents.
17. He loves his daughters.
18. He's active, not passive.
19. He's curious.
20. He can fix anything.

CONS

1. He weighs too much.
2. He lives in the Valley.

Well, I think that says it all.
"Come on, Ron Howard, let's go marry Big Johnson."

"When you realize you want to spend the rest of your life with somebody, you want the rest of your life to start as soon as possible."

—Harry Burns, *When Harry Met Sally*

Take Two

"WE ARE GATHERED here together," Harvey recited.

"No. No. No!" I interrupted. "Just get to the stuff that makes this legal."

As we stood on the balcony overlooking the bamboo trees Big Johnson had planted that year, a choir of crickets chirped in the background. The perfect soundtrack to our commitment symbolizing love and good luck while airplanes twinkled in the distant sky, taking off for a new destination. A whiff of eucalyptus mixed with hay enveloped us while Ron Howard stood beside me.

"Do you, Big Johnson, take Lisa to be your lawfully wedded wife?"

"I do."

"And do you, Lisa, take Big Johnson to be your lawfully wedded husband?"

My body tingled with excitement as I looked up at the sweetest, most loving, kind, generous, and bighearted man I'd ever known and said, "I do."

"You are my greatest adventure, and I almost missed it."

—Mr. Incredible, *The Incredibles*

The Ghoster's Encore

IN MY LATE fifties, now having been married to Big Johnson for a decade, living on his vineyard in Woodland Hills, I took a friend to my local drugstore to get her Covid booster shot. It was early morning, and there was only one pharmacist behind the counter. We checked in and took a seat in the small waiting area. We lost Ron Howard in 2013, so I brought Josie, my chocolate poodle mutt lapdog, to comfort my friend, who had anxiety with needles. Josie made us laugh as she twirled pirouettes for treats while we waited.

A voice with a familiar cadence spilled from the pharmacist window. A gray-haired man dressed in jeans and a button-down stood with his back to me. His thighs toned from running. His shoulders, broad, that tapered to a fit waist. A waist I had wrapped my arms around so many times a long time ago. I listened to him fill a prescription for his wife.

I didn't get up.

Instead, I watched him leave. Past the antacids and through the adult diaper aisle.

As I sat in that chair under bad fluorescent lighting, I hugged Josie tight and exhaled. I realized that the things that walk away from us are often the things that lead to life's greatest adventures. Had the Ghoster stayed, I never would have married Big Johnson, the man who has been there for me no matter what. Who loves and adores me. And who's given me my own happily ever after.

A Note Before We End

WE WERE INDEED married again later that evening, September 3, 2011, right before the cake cutting. When this book hits your favorite bookstore on September 22, 2026, we'll have been married fifteen years.

Things aren't always perfect, but I can't imagine a more perfect partner than Big Johnson.

For Lisa Cheek's wedding playlist,
please scan the code below.

Acknowledgments

THERE WOULD BE no book without the following:

Brooke Warner, my publisher, editor, and Wonder Woman Extraordinaire. Thank you for not giving up on this story. For being my mentor and modeling for me how to be a better person.

Erin O'Malley, my beloved and trusted beta reader.

Debbie Crawford, my copy editor.

Debi Key, my final eyes.

Aysu Selin, my travel and class buddy who's always up for a writer's adventure.

Susan Ito, Martha Frankel, Susan Brown, Deb Engle, Julie Cantrell, and Samantha Dunn for allowing me to jump into your classes so you could share your thoughts on how to make my story better.

So many writing groups: Dona, Sylvia, Susan, Barrie, Debi, Debbie, and Aysu.

Shannon Green and everyone at She Writes Press.

The followers of the *Becoming Mrs. Johnson* blog where this book began. Your enthusiasm encouraged me to dream bigger.

Caroline Gilman for making my social media sparkle.

Ron Howard, Josephine Simon, Alvin, and Lil Elvis Bruce Wayne, my adorable dogs who have taught me how to love.

And most of all Big Johnson, my biggest, greatest love. Thank you for making my life so big and showing me how to be loved.

Every day is a big day. Celebrate and savor each one.

About the Author

LISA CHEEK'S is an author and former film and television editor known for her humorous, candid writing about relationships and identity. Her debut memoir, *Sit, Cinderella, Sit*, was a *People Magazine* pick, an Amazon bestseller, a Next Generation Indie Book Award finalist, and was named one of Zibby Media's Most Anticipated Books of 2025. Her latest memoir, *The Big Day*, is a funny, unflinching look at love, marriage, and the complicated question of whether to stay or walk away. You can find her musings at *One Minute Thoughts From A Pink Head* on Substack. She lives in Los Angeles with two dogs, two cats, and her husband, Big Johnson, where she has several scripts in various stages of development while working on her next memoir.

Author photo © Charlie Nunn Photography